DÉCORS BARBARES

For Juliette

DÉCORS BARBARES

THE ENCHANTING INTERIORS OF

NATHALIE FARMAN-FARMA

VENDOME
NEW YORK • LONDON

FOREWORD

Once you have been young together, nothing and no one can take that away. One of the most satisfying experiences—making old age bearable to me—has been watching certain friends from early life find their way to great success. Among this small club there are some chefs, some fashion designers, some movie producers—even a writer or two. Most are still buddies. In design, and in friendship, foremost among them is Nathalie Farman-Farma.

Nathalie and I became close in Paris in autumn of 1990. This was just after she graduated from college, and she was a hard creature to peg—an American girl from Greenwich and California, very beautiful and very wholesome, who also spoke fluent French. She came from a high-achieving background of stolid aesthetics yet had an enthusiasm for taste and style—and, as it turned out, an instinct which seemed to have sprung fully formed. As we walked the streets of Paris getting to know the lost world of Madeleine Castaing (her shop was still open on the Rue Jacob) and the avant-garde of Frédéric Méchiche (his had just opened in the Marais), we spoke in shorthand, laughed continuously, and respected each other's eye for quality.

What stood out most about her then and now were two character traits: her loyalty and her total non-tolerance of phonies. I think these are essential to her success in conjuring the taste you see in these pages—an original take on the colors and romantic atmosphere of the nineteenth century—for she is loyal to what she loves and refuses to dilute her inspirations to conform or pander to the contemporary. Like Nureyev and Zeffirelli, she likes her nineteenth century fresh, and makes us see it that way, too.

Hannah Arendt | The Origins of Totalitarianism
ALBUM LEWIS CARROLL
ALBUM AYMÉ
ALBUM ARAGON
COLETTE ŒUVRES
COLETTE ŒUVRES
PAUL VALÉRY ŒUVRES
PAUL VALÉRY ŒUVRES
ANDRÉ GIDE ROMANS
BORGES ŒUVRES COMPLÈTES
They Were Counted
They Were Divided
BÁNFFY The PHOENIX LAND
Radetzky March
JOSEPH ROTH
PIERRE VIDAL-NAQUET
Les juifs, la mémoire et le
Gustave Flaubert
ELISABETH VIGÉE LE BRUN
PIERRE VIDAL-NAQUET
VICHY FRANCE
The Ancien Régime
Selected Poems
BIRDS, BEASTS AND FLOWERS!
GEORGES SIMENON
WHISTLER
ABSINTHE
Gaudí
Auguste Rodin en México
Mahomet à Charlemagne

As you know if you are holding this book, Nathalie today has developed one of the most passionate and sophisticated eyes in the world. We can trace this virtuosity using point-to-point navigation from the "light bulb" moment in the Rue Jacob, to the extraordinary point of view she brought to her New York apartment on Ninth Street a decade later, to the even more developed and sure-handed style of the house in London where she lives now. Ninth Street was a lab—a rehearsal for what has since come. What started as a friend offering a helping hand turned into one of the most poetic and sophisticated projects I have ever been a part of. (To this day I have never had a client tell me to make them a room "where Tolstoy would want to spent the night.") Many pieces we acquired for this apartment, like a brass bed from the old Adlon Hotel in Berlin, are still well-loved and can be found in this book, telling new stories.

Nathalie comes from a family of charming and forthright women. Most fiery of these was her sister Juliette, who left us much too soon. I know that Juliette's advice and counsel was essential to the development of Décors Barbares, and also to the courage required of Nathalie to take her unique voice and enter the textile business in the first place. Look for her spirit in these pages, in the passionate colors and conjuring of Old Russian style. It's a family trait. But the most important thing is all Nathalie's own: that to really be an alchemist—to harness the romance that can turn Lake Tahoe into a dacha and Greenwich into a Proustian dream—you can't ask for a map, or anyone's permission. You just have to be authentic.

David Netto

INTRODUCTION

With hindsight I can see that I was always sensitive to the power of atmospheric rooms. However, it was only later in life, after I started a family, that I became involved in the art of interiors, and specifically textiles. My taste, initially, was very disciplined and French, but once I met my husband, Amir, who is from Iran, I began experimenting with more freedom. When I decorated our first home the guiding vision was to create a mood that incorporated East and West. I was particularly inspired by the mix of patterns and colors in Persian miniatures and the tribal robes of Central Asia. The more I looked East, the more I lost the fear of things not going together. I wanted to change the rules. Unable to find the fabrics I wanted I decided to start my own line, Décors Barbares, which makes bold prints that have the feel of vintage textiles.

I started to look for aesthetic connections between East and West. I read and I traveled. I delved into the Great Game, the Silk Road, the Ballets Russes. What was immediately clear was that there are no compass points when is comes to style. Fabrics, porcelain, rugs, costume, fashion, jewelry—all attest to the fluidity of design in a continuous cycle of mutual influence. As I started to collect material for use as visual references I became more attuned to the small variations of pattern in objects that have a similar origin and purpose, such as Russian headscarves. Comparing pieces that are linked but discrete is a way to deepen knowledge and see patterns as living and perpetually evolving, and therefore essential to the creative process.

In this book I have tried to explore some of these ideas and also share sources of inspiration. It is the journal of an excavation into what makes taste personal. It is also an exhortation to see pattern as one of the most beautiful expressions of human connectivity.

THE STUDIO

PARIS
MOSCOW
LEON BAKST
THE AGE OF DIAGHILEV
RUSSIAN
NATALIA GONCHAROVA
GONCHAROVA
FROM RUSSIA
MUSÉE RUSSE
ÉPOQUE ET SON STYLE
Them
SONIA DELAUNAY
POIRET
Serge Poliakoff
STALINGRAD
ICONS

WORKING WITH FABRICS

"I find the innocence and creativity in folk costumes very inspiring. Every region has its own distinctive and recognizable traditions, but there are universal elements beyond the time and style."

Tucked away behind my London home, on a genteel side street in the once semi-rural artistic enclave of Chelsea, is a pair of identical Victorian purpose-built studios, each with a north-facing skylight and a room large enough for the original owner to work on outsized canvasses or sculptures. Now opened up to create one space, this is where I design my fabrics, and where I keep my books on design, on Russia, on ethnographic photography, as well as piles of costumes and textiles. Every morning I cross the threshold and enter into another world—barbarian territory.

I chose to name my business Décors Barbares in homage to the Ballets Russes, a consistent source of inspiration for my decorating and design, and still a relevant aesthetic exploration of the relationship between East and West. When the Russian impresario Sergei Diaghilev arrived in Paris in 1909 and put together his troupe of Russian musicians and dancers, he was already capitalizing on a fever for Eastern exoticism. Many adjectives were used to describe the Russian "invasion": primitive, savage, oriental, wild, instinctual, pagan, but the most frequent epithet was barbarian. In the words of the French art critic Jean-Louis Vaudoyer, who often accompanied Marcel Proust to see Ballets Russes productions: "Having remained barbarians in a Europe whose every fiber is civilized, the Russians now have the most richly creative, beautifully developed inner selves. As fresh, avid and sincere as children, they give themselves over entirely and search their souls feverishly. They are not hindered by conventions."

The Russian spirit seemed to encapsulate everything that Belle Époque France was not, and Diaghilev astutely doubled-down on the prevailing desire for escapism. His triumphal first season included the "Polovtsian Dances," a ballet set in the encampment of a nomadic Turkic tribe. But there was always more to Diaghilev than crowd-pleasing sensationalism. He was also introducing the culture of the steppes, relatively unknown outside of Russia. The costumes designed by Nicholas Roerich for the Polovtsians included authentic silk ikats and braids purchased in Russia, homage to the beauty of Central Asian patterns and colors. More than a century later, Diaghilev's Ballets Russes continue to inspire. The secret of their lasting originality lies in the freedom to mix influences combined with a commitment to respect cultures of the past—an ethos that guides my own work with fabrics.

Князь Синодал
оп. Демонъ

BALLETS RUSSES

Perhaps no designer has ever reached such heights of fame as Léon Bakst at the time of his association with the Ballets Russes, and never more so than with the opulent costumes and sets he created for the 1910 production of *Schéhérazade*, an orientalist fantasy based on *The Thousand and One Nights*.

As the society portraitist Jacques-Émile Blanche commented: "The first performance of *Schéhérazade* was an important event for the theater, for the dressmakers, for interior decorators, for jewelers and all branches of decoration. It is difficult today to realize the metamorphosis that transformed the decorative arts."

Indeed, the fashionable women of the time rushed to be dressed in turbans and harem pants like those offered up by the couturier Paul Poiret, whose designs epitomize the then craze for Eastern splendor. Poiret denied any influence from Bakst. Nonetheless, for the launch of his spring 1911 collection he invited *le tout-Paris* to a Persian ball. The legendary Marchesa Luisa Casati, who embodied fin-de-siècle extravagance, commissioned flamboyant Oriental-style outfits from Bakst himself.

I looked at Bakst in a new light when I noticed many of his costumes were inspired by Qajar paintings from Iran. Even the poses of dancers in some of his sketches echo depictions of Persian dancers. To my knowledge, very little else links Western culture and nineteenth century Persian art, Paris, and Tehran. Under Diaghilev, Russia became intermediary to the East.

Indeed, the issue of Russia's Eastern character was always part of the intellectual debate around how "Russianness" was defined. The very bulk of Russia's landmass is in Asia, and the sense of a shared heritage long linked Russians with Turkic and Persian culture. Mongol or Tartar ancestry was a lineage to take pride in. This is what drew me to the Russian aesthetic in the first place—it did not easily fit the pattern of other European forms of Orientalism.

LES BALLETS RUSSES
AU
THÉATRE DU CHATELET
BAKST
1911
Pour le costume de "La Péri"

Aquarelle de Léon BAKST

pour le Costume de "LA PÉRI"

BALLETS RUSSES
THE STOCKHOLM COLLECTION
THE BALLETS RUSSES and the Art of Design
Léon Bakst The Art of Theatre and Dance
КОЛЛЕКЦИЯ ЛОБАНОВЫХ-РОСТОВСКИХ
MASTERPIECES of RUSSIAN STAGE DESIGN 1880-1930
Volume I
John E. Bowlt, Nina and Nikita D. Lobanov-Rostovsky, and Olga Shaumyan
ANTIQUE COLLECTORS' CLUB
ENCYCLOPEDIA of RUSSIAN STAGE DESIGN 1880-1930
Volume II
John E. Bowlt, Nina and Nikita D. Lobanov-Rostovsky
ANTIQUE COLLECTORS' CLUB
Jane Pritchard
LES BALLETS RUSSES DE DIAGHILEV
LEON BAKST CHARLES SPENCER ST. MARTIN'S PRESS
LEON BAKST AND THE BALLETS RUSSES CHARLES SPENCER
ACADEMY
THE AGE OF DIAGHILEV
PALACE EDITIONS
CHARLES SPENCER LEON BAKST
Musée de Montmartre RUSSES
FRAGMENTS EDITIONS
ALEXANDER VOLKOV: OF SAND AND SILK
CHRISTIE'S
Russian Legends Folk Tales and Fairy Tales
GRONINGER MUSEUM NAI PUBLISHERS
ART INTO PRODUCTION MUSEUM OF MODERN ART OXFORD/CRAFTS COUNCIL
PARIS MOSCOU
KUNST UND REVOLUTION ART AND REVOLUTION
Russische und Sowjetische Kunst 1910–1932
Russian and Soviet Art 1910–1932
GRONINGER MUSEUM
WORKING FOR DIAGHILEV
RUSSIAN MODERNISM: CROSS-CURRENTS OF GERMAN AND RUSSIAN ART, 1907–1917
PRESTEL
NEUE GALERIE NEW YORK
L'Avant-Garde russe
L'ABITO DELLA RIVOLUZIONE
AVANGUARDIA RUSSA
ESPERIENZE DI UN MONDO NUOVO
NEW WORLD EXPERIENCE
Sotheby's LONDON RUSSIAN AND SOVIET PORCELAIN, 1825–1985
СОВЕТСКИЙ ФАРФОР
ПОДНЕСЕНИЕ К РОЖДЕСТВУ
РУДОЛЬФ ВИЛЬДЕ (1868–1938) · ФАРФОР. СТЕКЛО
ONARY CERAMICS
CIRCLING THE SQUARE
BLAKESLEY & SAMU From REALISM to the SILVER AGE
PEINTRES ET VOYAGEURS RUSSES DU XIXe SIÈCLE
Sotheby's LONDON RUSSIAN PICTURES · РУССКОЕ ИСКУССТВО
Z. SEREBRIAKOVA
VALKENIER ILYA REPIN
Sotheby's RUSSIAN BOOKS, MANUSCRIPTS, MAPS AND PHOTOGRAPHS
MACDOUGALL'S RUSSIAN ART
Bernard J Shapero Rare Books RUSSIA
MUDEC
Il cavaliere errante
In viaggio verso l'astrazione
KANDINSKIJ
RUSSIAN LANDSCAPE
SSM THE RUSSIAN AVANT-GARDE
RUSSIA AND THE ARTS ROSALIND P. BLAKESLEY
RUSSIAN AND SOVIET PAINTINGS 1900-19
The Peredvizhniki
ation russe en photos · 1917-1947
E RUSSE EN EXIL · EUROPE · 1917-1947
RUSSIAN PARIS

COSTUME REVOLUTION
Trefoil
YASINSKAYA SOVIET TEXTILE DESIGN OF THE REVOLUTIONARY PERIOD
YASINSKAYA SOVIET TEXTILE DESIGN OF THE REVOLUTIONARY PERIOD
RED STAR OVER RUSSIA DAVID KING
TATE
INSIDE THE RAINBOW
RUSSIAN CHILDREN'S LITERATURE 1920–35: BEAUTIFUL BOOKS, TERRIBLE TIMES
Peter Noever Ed. RODCHENKO · STEPANOVA
PRESTEL
The Russian Avant-garde, Siberia and the East
Skira
DECTER NICHOLAS ROERICH
EDITED BY MATTHEW GALE AND NATALIA SIDLINA
NATALIA GONCHAROVA
THE RUSSIAN THEATRE FÜLÖP-MILLER & GREGOR
HARRAP
Soviet Impressionist Painting
Vern G. Swanson
ANTIQUE COLLECTORS' CLUB
Schouvaloff The Art of
Yale
FROM RUSSIA WITH LOVE
Athenaeum
Teatro della Ragione / Teatro del Desiderio
L'Arte di Alexandre Benois e Léon Bakst
Centre national de la danse
DANS LE SILLAGE DES BA
de la beauté
Vassil
Tatiana Mojenok - Ninin
Bonhams
SOVIET WOMEN AND THEIR
SOTHEBY'S London
Blakesley and Reid RUSSIAN ART AND THE WEST
Northern Illinois
KACHURIN SOVIET TEXTILES
IGOR SAVITSKY Artist, Collector, Museum Founder
by Marinika Babanazarova
MODA E DESIGN IN RUSS
OLOGRAF EDIZIONI
VIET COSTUME AND TEXTILES 1917-1945
EVGENIA KIRICHENKO • COMPILED BY MIKHAIL ANIKST
Flammarion
ABR
Rosalind P. Blakesley The Russian Canvas
Jeanine Warnod SERGE FÉRAT Un Cubiste russe à Paris
Éditions d'art Aurora Léningrad VENETSIANOV et son école
BUILDING THE REVOLUTION SOVIET ART AND ARCHITECTURE 1915–1935
FROM RUSS
REVOLUTION Russian Art 1917–1932
DAVID JACKSON THE RUSSIAN VISION THE ART OF ILYA REPIN
Valentin SEROV
The Russian Vision THE ART OF ILYA REPIN DAVID JACKSON
Сергей Виноградов
NATALIA GONCHAROVA THE RUSSIAN
GONCHAROVA The Art and Design of Natalia Goncharova
Anthony Parton
The First Master of Russian Painting Valentin SEROV
L'Art russe dans la seconde moitié du XIXe siècle : en quête d'identité
MUSÉE RUSSE
АЛЛА РУСАКОВА ЗИНАИДА СЕРЕБРЯКОВА
ВАЛЕНТИН СЕРОВ
Toustavéli Le Chevalier à la peau de panthère
CHRISTIE'S LONDON RUSSIAN ART

GEORGIAN COSTUME

I am fascinated by areas of frontier, lands where aesthetic influences collide. Few are as storied and magical as the Caucasus, a mountain range straight out of a fable by Luis Borges. It divides Europe and Asia, West and East. By virtue of its seclusion and inaccessibility, it is one of the richest geographical regions for cultural and linguistic variety. There are accounts of tribes on opposite sides of the same valley who speak a different language and have a different religion. Instead of being a melting pot, the Caucasus became a refuge where small groups of people have been able to maintain their ethnic identity—even under the sporadic domination of the Persian, Ottoman, and Russian empires.

The traditional costumes of the region are as varied and colorful as the languages. They are recognizably unique to the Caucasus, yet carry echoes of Byzantine, Medieval, and Safavid dress. I have assembled a collection of men's tunics from Khevsureti, a remote province in the high valleys in the north of Georgia. The *talavari*, as it is called, is made of dark hand-woven wool and has slits on both sides for horse riding. It is worn by Khevsur men together with a niello belt and dagger. Front and back are lavishly embroidered and adorned with beads, white buttons, coins, and other silver ornaments. Some have appliquéd triangular designs made of colorful fabric, which remind me of Ballets Russes costumes.

The striking element of the *talavari* is the exceptionally refined embroidery of cross symbols, often interlocking. The crosses are all square, like the Greek, Jerusalem, and Maltese crosses. This led early ethnographers to believe the Khevsur people could be traced back to the Crusaders, especially since they still wore chainmail in the nineteenth century. However compelling the theory, it has long been dispelled. It is more probable that the Khevsur crosses are ancient solar symbols transposed to a Christian age.

BLOOD & CHAMPAGNE
NIKO PIROSMANI
Matisse in the Studio
KAZIMIR MALÉVITCH
COUTURE

CHANTS
BALLETS
TABLEAUX
VIVANTS
THÉATRE
D'ART RUSSE
PRÉSENTÉ PAR
Russian Houses
DUCHAMP
Picasso and Portraiture
JEAN BÉRAUD
THE ANATOMY OF COLOUR
JAMES TISSOT
SARGENT
GEORGES DE LA TOUR
Balthus
ISABELLA

COQ D'OR
CHANTS
BALLETS
TABLEAUX
VIVANTS
THÉATRE
D'ART RUSSE
PRÉSENTÉ PAR
ANATOLE DOLINOFF
"Succès"
H. CHACHOIN Imp. PARIS_1928

MONDES TSIGANES
les Nabis & le décor
IRANIAN-RUSSIAN ENCOUNTERS
BLOOD & CHAMPAGNE
NIKO PIROSMANI
Matisse in the Studio
ANI SMITH
KAZIMIR MA

folio essais Simone de Beauvoir Le deuxième sexe I
Henry Rousso Le syndrome de Vichy
Histoire
Sartre Les mots
Stendhal Lucien Leuwen
Racine
Œuvres de Voltaire
Histoire de Charles XII
Le Mur
Sartre
Caligula
Albert Camus
Contes de fées
Stendhal The Red and The Black
Michel Foucault
histoire de la folie à l'âge classique
André Gide L'immoraliste
E. Rostand
Cyrano de Bergerac
L'Aiglon
786
Le deuxième sexe II
Frederic Morton
Aux Assises
Zola The Earth
Maigret à Vichy
Georges Simenon
Emmanuel Carrère Limonov
Emmanuel Carrère Un roman russe
The Age of Revolution 1789-1848 · E.J. Hobsbawm
Saint-Just Théorie politique
La Peste
Camus
Friedrich Nietzsche
The Birth of Tragedy and The Genealogy of Morals
Anchor Books
Cocteau sur le rivage
the French Revolution
Elisabeth Vigée Le Brun
C. B. A. Behrens
Ernest Renan
Œuvres complètes
Mauriac
Le Noeud de vipères

Life of Voltaire
Tallentyre
VOLTAIRE
LES MYSTÈRES DE PARIS
ALEXANDRE DUMAS
Marcel Proust
PROUST'S DUCHESS
CAROLINE WEBER
Le Musée imaginaire de Marcel Proust
DUMAS
Les Trois Mousquetaires
Vingt ans après
Le monde de Proust vu par Paul Nadar
BLACK COUNT
TOM REISS
THE EMBRACE OF UNREASON
FRANCE, 1914–1940
FREDERICK BROWN
CITIZENS
SIMON SCHAMA
LIETUVIŲ LIAUDIES MOTERŲ DRABUŽIAI XVIII a. pab.–XX a. pr.

ЛѢСНЫЕ

COLORS OF THE SILK ROAD

A chapan is a brightly colored robe worn throughout Central Asia by men and women from all walks of life. A prized indicator of status, it was traditionally offered as a gift to important guests. No two chapans are alike. Some are made from opulent fabrics, brocades, silk and velvet ikats; others from cheaper cloth. They are trimmed with a woven geometric band to ward off evil, and sometimes, among the Turkmen, tassels and charms are added for extra protection.

The lure of the chapan resides in the brightly printed cotton lining that clashes with the exterior of the coat, creating a joyful juxtaposition of pattern and color. From the mid-nineteenth century through to Soviet times these prints were, for the most part, manufactured in Russian factories specifically for export to Central Asia, or Turkestan as it was then known. Their designs reveal a blend of Eastern and Western influences, and celebrate the rich history of the Silk Road.

From China to the Mediterranean, the Silk Road linked all the cultures of Asia with distant Europe. Like a great oceanic current, this network of trade posts with dusty bazaars, tea houses and caravanserais conveyed a two-way flow of goods and ideas through impossible landscapes. It was subjected to waves of invasion by nomadic tribes driven west out of Siberia. Yet when one of these tribes—such as the Mongols under Genghis Khan—was able to establish lasting rule and stability in Central Asia, the region was not only at the heart of international trade, but the center of multicultural sophistication.

We are lucky enough to have a rich archive of ethnographic photography on Central Asia, not least of which are the early color photographs of Sergei Prokudin-Gorskii, who was granted permission by Tsar Nicholas II to travel throughout the Russian Empire to document regional customs. He visited Central Asia in 1911 and took portraits of a wide variety of people, from the street vendors of Samarkand to the Emir of Bukhara, all seen wearing their chapans.

Рис. 3.

Рис. 4.

гельск. музей

Русск. ручная набойка.

COLLECTING PATTERNS

With fabrics, I am always on the hunt for traces of the past that I can bring back to life. So much is happenstance, and I am often reminded of how accidental the preservation of textile documents can be. Great designs can be found in a patchwork quilt, the hem of a skirt or the lining of a sleeve.

Antique clothing is a wonderful primary source and the best way to reach into folkloric traditions. This had led me to collect Russian headscarves—particularly the nineteenth-century calicos and block prints that have either an indigo blue ground or a madder red ground. Factory-made, these were cheaper than traditional textiles. Initially there was a strong French influence on the design, but as their popularity grew, variations and combinations of patterns spread until a vernacular unique to Russia had been created.

Representations of textiles in art can sometimes be as interesting as the artifacts themselves. Sometimes I will come across an unusual item, such as an album of hand-painted illustrations of pattern designs. The artist had traveled to Arkhangelsk in the 1950s to research old Russian fabrics. This type of document, where another pair of eyes has selected an item of interest, is most valuable to me since I get a glimpse into the past. It is helpful to glean how the fabrics were perceived in a Russian context. This is why I go back again and again to book illustrators or costume designers who paid close attention to historical textiles, particularly Léon Bakst, Nicholas Roerich, and Ivan Bilibin.

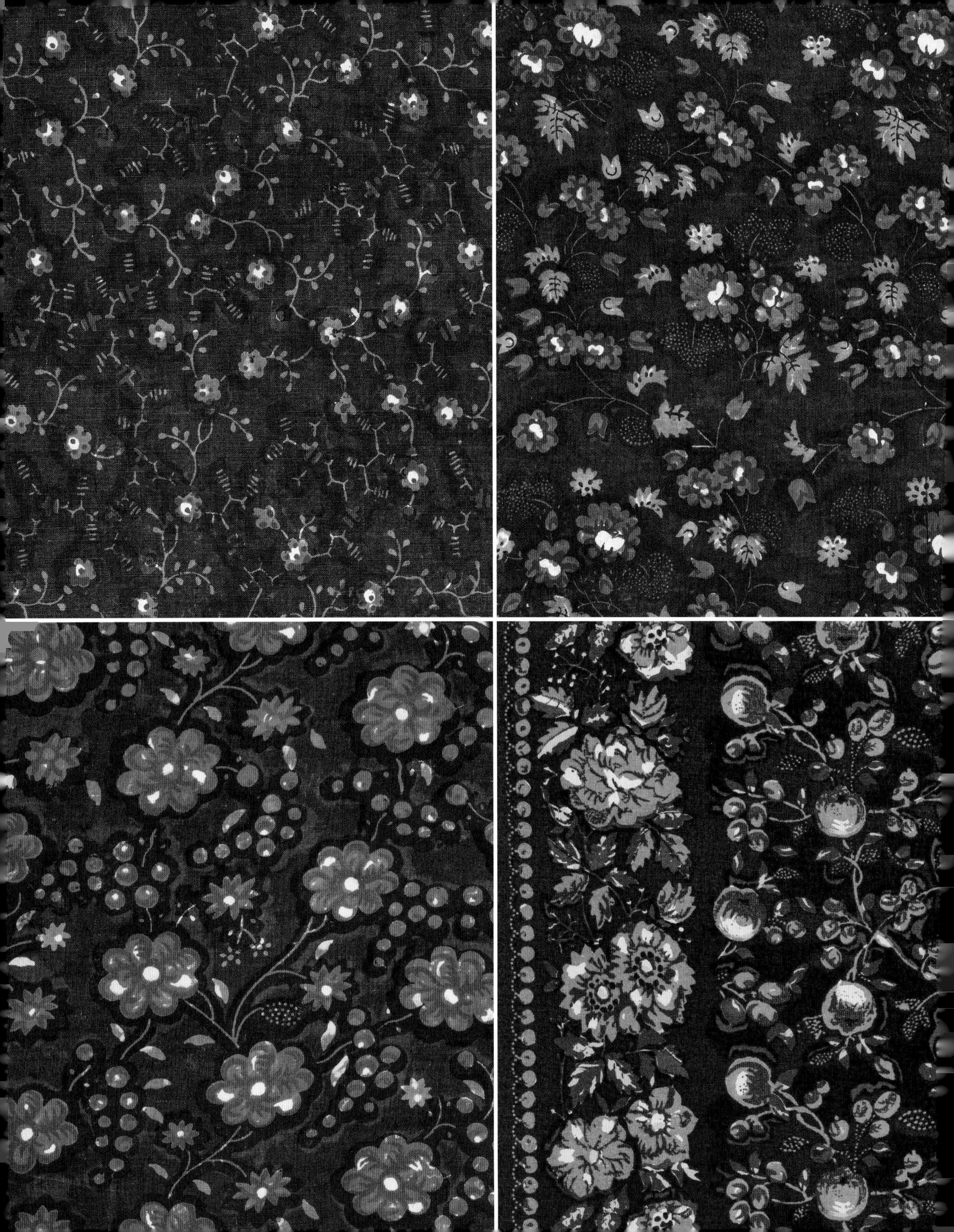

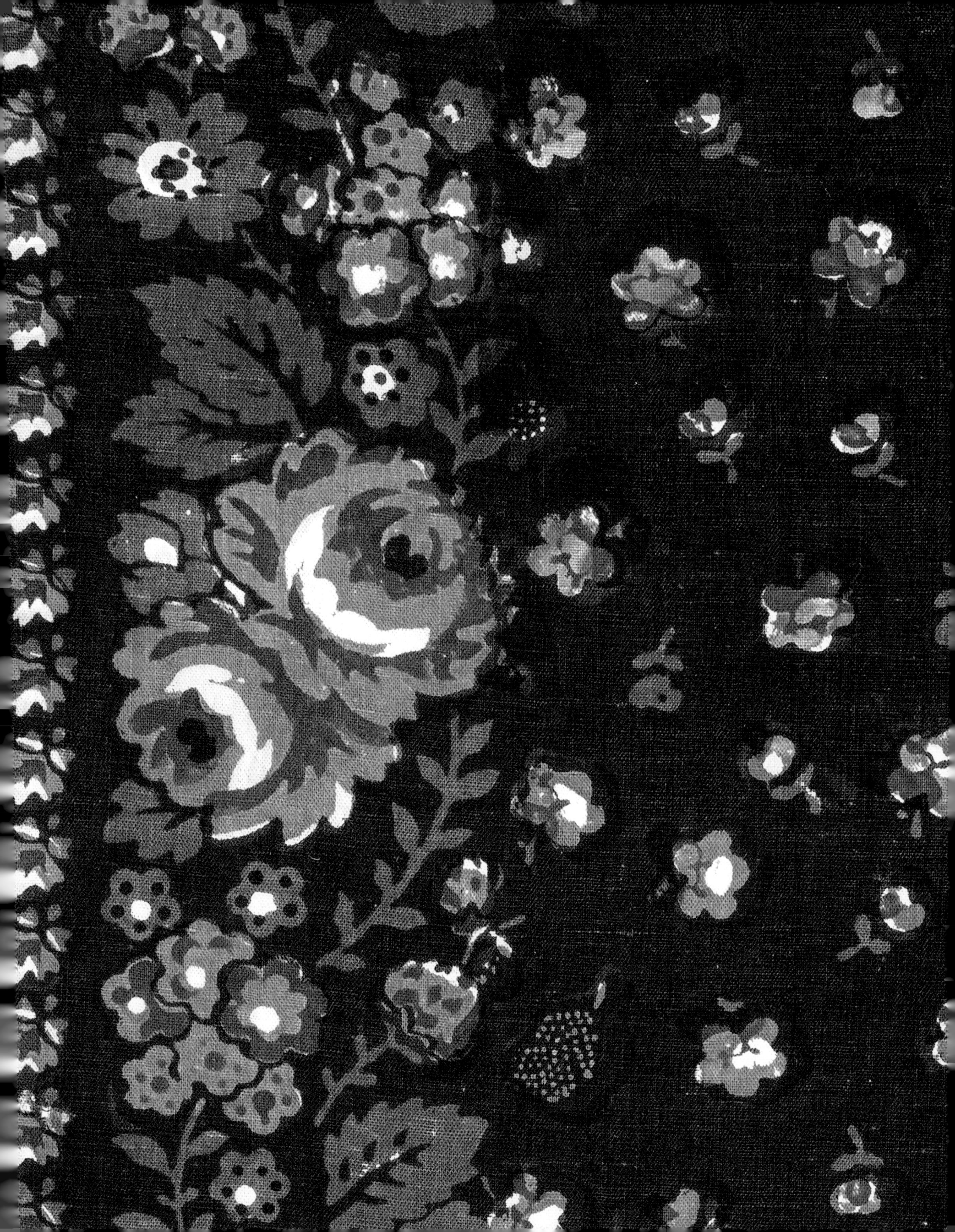

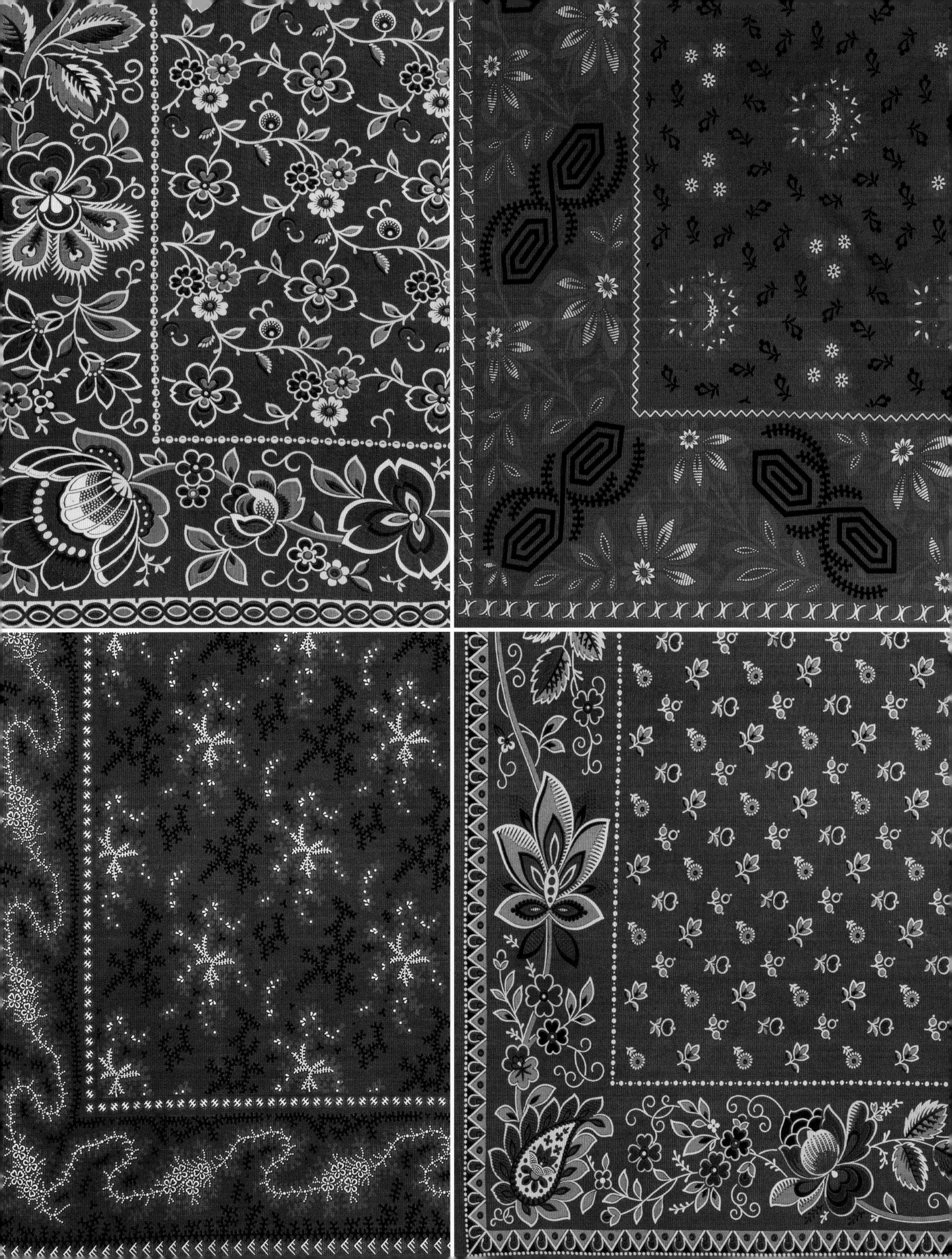

MOUCHOIRS
imprimés
879 & 1880

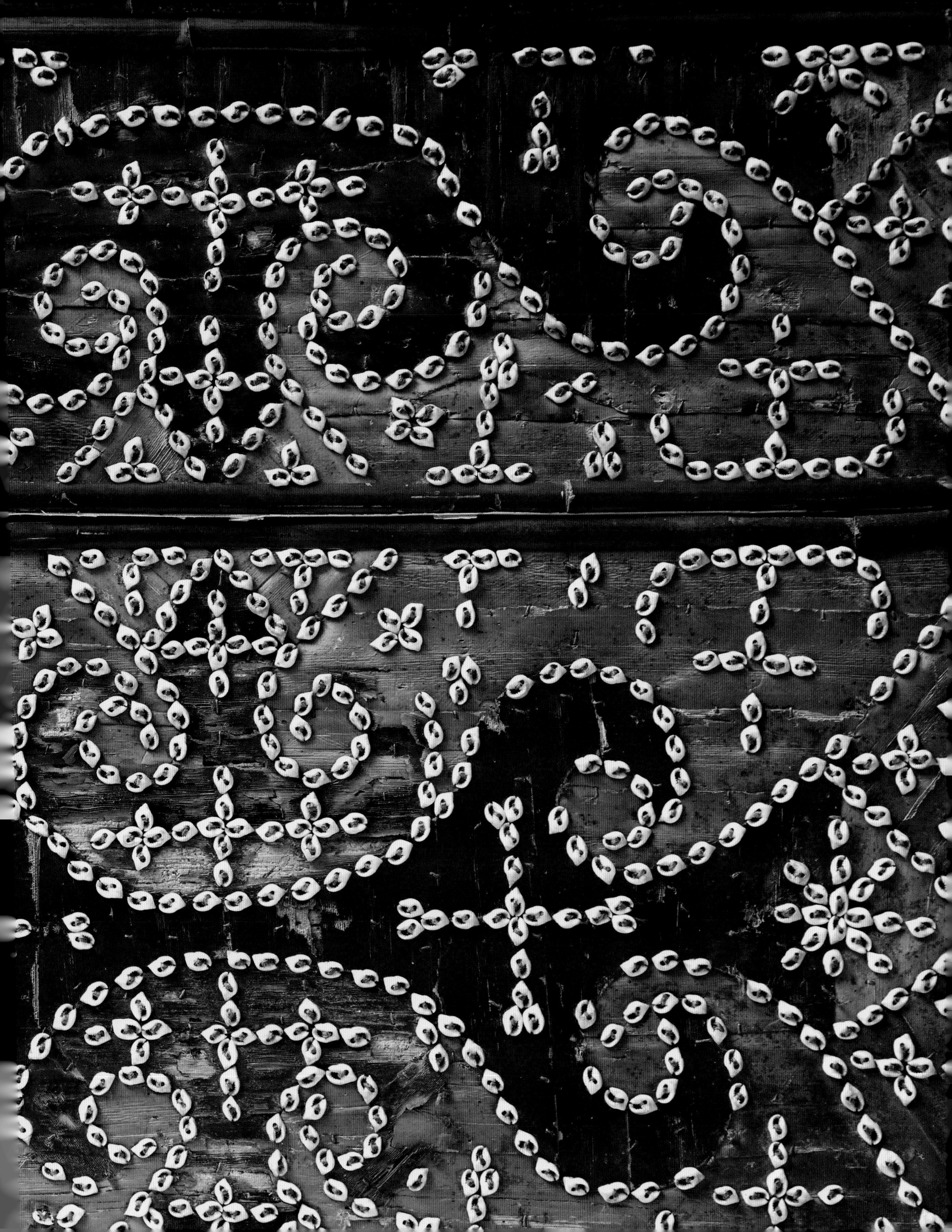

TAHOE

CHILDHOOD INSPIRATIONS

There is really nothing in adult life to compare to the joy children feel when school breaks up for the summer holiday. Suddenly there is freedom, and time to explore the world. It is like a journey to an exotic and magical land. In my case, this magical land was Lake Tahoe in the Sierra Nevada mountains of California. The landscape lends itself to adventures, with tall trees casting impossibly long shadows across the dirt roads, the cabins, and the lake. The days are cloudless, and the night sky throws out bright stars.

All these years later, there is still nothing I would rather do than spend time with my extended family in Tahoe. The house has big common spaces for meals, conversations, guitar playing, and all sorts of games, while little cabins scattered about the grounds provide a retreat for those in need of quiet. The exposed-beam library is the first room I really fell in love with, and where I understood the impact a decorated space could have on the imagination. It has an imposing brick fireplace crowned by a moose head; otherwise, it is all windows onto the forest, and bookshelves. These are filled with novels, histories, memoirs, and Agatha Christie's murder mysteries—a somewhat motley assortment of tastes. I was told that some of the books were once purchased by the pound for decorative purposes. Grand and rustic, slightly out of time, the effect is enchanting. As a child, I found it the perfect setting for make-believe. I was often an archaeologist in search of artifacts from lost civilizations.

This association between books and the majestic untamed wilderness of the American West led me to a lasting love of nineteenth-century Russian novels, in which, more often than not, nature and life in remote rural Russia are at the heart of the hero's quest to understand life. It was in this library that I first discovered Pushkin and then Lermontov, Tolstoy, Turgenev, Chekhov—all authors who shepherded me into adulthood. As I walked from cabin to cabin, I often imagined the dirt roads would take me to a neighbor's dacha.

Those paths, which I wandered so freely, led to an inner world that became the source of my visual iconography. This blending of the real and the written, a fusion of the material and the make-believe, is something I carry with me to this day.

"Tahoe is a Washoe name, meaning 'Big Waters.' As a child I used to love looking for arrowheads along the shore, with the sad knowledge that a way of life had disappeared forever on the lake."

KING HENRY VI. PART II.
MUCH ADO ABOUT NOTHING
CORIOLANUS
NIGHT
A MIDSUMMER NIGHT
ERICLES
MEO AND JULIET
TITUS ANDRONICUS

HAMLET
VENUS & ADONIS
THE SONNETS
TIMON OF ATHENS
ANTONY & CLEOPATRA
THE MERRY WIVES OF WINDSOR
AS YOU LIKE IT
KING RICHARD III.

LIN YUTANG
MY COUNTRY AND MY PEOPLE
THE MAN WITH MY FACE
Samuel W. Taylor
THE CORPSE IN THE CORNER SALOON
Hampton Stone
MURDER IS MUTUEL
Jack Dolph
THE LATE UNLAMENTED
R. A. J. Walling
SHOES FOR MY LOVE
Joan Leslie
DEAD SURE
Stewart Sterling
FRAMED IN GUILT
Day Keene
A ROPE FOR THE BARON
Anthony Morton
THE BLACK COAT
C. & G. Little
GIFT OF DEATH
Edward Ronns
A KILLER IS LOOSE AMONG US
Robert Terrall
THE CASE OF WILLIAM SMITH
Patricia Wentworth
ST. IVES
ROBERT LOUIS STEVENSON
SCRIBNERS
ZLATEH THE GOAT
Harper & Row
TIMES A HISTORY OF THE EARLY WORLD
BREASTED
SECOND EDITION
GINN AND COMPANY
A PASSAGE TO INDIA
E.M. FORSTER
HARCOURT BRACE & CO.
LIBRARY OF THE WORLD'S BEST LITERATURE
VOL.V
VOL.VI
When lights go out
Have these about
So You're Going to England!
LAUGHLIN
Houghton Mifflin Company
Do Not Murder Before Christmas

SIBERIAN ARTIFACT

A few years ago I purchased a pair of tall reindeer-hide snow boots from a Finnish dealer who specializes in shamanic artifacts. They were worn by the North Khanty (Ostyak) people of northern Siberia. The short horizontal stripes are made of felt and identify the wearer's tribe and gender. Even simple items such as footwear display a great deal of regional and cultural diversity in ornamentation.

Like many other semi-nomadic tribes of Siberia, the Khanty live on hunting, fishing, and reindeer herding, and they worship animal spirits. This belief in harmony between the human and animal world links the indigenous people of both Siberia and North America. Through the Bering Straits they have a strong bond of shared ancestry and a shared eco-system.

The poetry of Native American life was eloquently captured in the black and white photographs of Edward Curtis during the late nineteenth and early twentieth centuries. And still today, the films of my friend Hamid Sardar document the reindeer herders of Mongolia. I have such respect for adventurers who, like them and many others in between, have recorded a way of life as it disappears. Aside from the boots, the library in Tahoe has a few small talismanic objects that pay homage to this ancient wisdom: a pair of Sioux turtle fetishes and some Inuit carved walrus ivory figurines, which were probably used as toys.

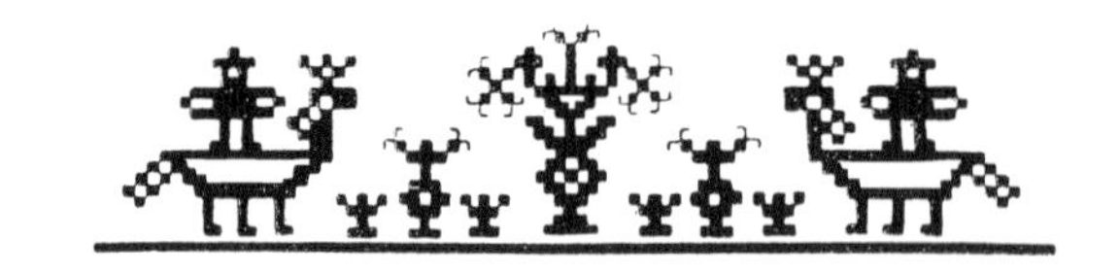

THE WRITER'S HANDBOOK
BURMA SURGEON
BLACK LAMB AND GREY FALCON
RELIGION AND MEDICINE
WORCESTER McCOMB CORIAT
THE WATCH THAT ENDS THE NIGHT
EARLY HAVOC
A PENKNIFE IN MY HEART
WASHINGTON IRVING'S WORKS
SALMAGUNDI
LUCY CROWN
THE REFORMATION
THE UNFORGIVEN
SILVER PLATTER
DON'T GO NEAR THE WATER
AFTER YOU MARCO POLO
DICTIONARY of ERRORS
THE HEART ON THE SLEEVE

ETHNOGRAPHIC TYPES

The first attempt to catalog the various people in the Russian Empire dates back to 1776 with Johann Gottlieb Georgi's *A Description of All the Nationalities That Inhabit the Russian State*. The Russian edition was dedicated to Catherine the Great, who had commissioned the work. Georgi was a German botanist and geographer who was a student of Carl Linnaeus, but he is best remembered for his engravings depicting the costumes and customs of the many ethnic groups that lived in Russia. The vast expanse ruled by the tsarina stretched from the Gulf of Finland to the steppes of Central Asia and from the Caspian Sea to the boreal forests of Siberia. Georgi pioneered Russian ethnography and many intrepid scientists and artists followed in his steps. My favorite is Theodore de Pauly, whose 1862 *Peoples of Russia* (dedicated to Alexander II) renders the fabrics worn by the tsar's subjects in lavish detail.

In 1779 the Imperial Porcelain factory created the "Peoples of Russia," a series of porcelain figurines based on Georgi's drawings. These figurines with their colorful costumes were produced in a collectible series and became wildly popular. They were also a canny propaganda tool for a government trying to incorporate disparate groups into an expanding empire. Such was the enduring interest in these porcelain characters that variations on this series were still being manufactured during Soviet times.

QUEEN of FRANCE

UNO
MONOPOLY
Clue MASTER DETECTIVE
Clue MASTER DETECTIVE

ROMANTIC FLORALS

Many of my fabrics came to life with the idea of using them one day at the lake house, linking the outdoors and indoors with wild flowers and the motion of swaying grasses. It is my way of paying homage to the ever-present beauty of nature up in the mountains. Furthermore, botanical prints soften a room and create a sense of painterliness; I have long admired the richly patterned interiors of Édouard Vuillard and Pierre Bonnard, two French artists who captured so well the poetry of every-day life.

My floral designs are drawn from an eclectic array of textile documents in my collection. Été Moscovite is a pattern based on a nineteenth-century print from Pavlovsky Posad, the legendary center of the Russian shawl industry outside of Moscow, while Véra is constructed from two-inch-wide fragments of chintz found in a Central Asian patchwork. At first I thought I could piece together the original pattern as a fabric puzzle of sorts, but ultimately there were too many gaps and I filled in the missing elements with new ones. The rich Russian color schemes work well with wooden walls.

Simple linens also have a place. My favorite bedroom in Tahoe has windows on three sides, so I chose a pattern with a little flower sprig, Polonaise. This design was inspired by the apron of a Polish folkloric costume from the Seweryn Udziela Ethnographic Museum in Krakow. I had taken a picture of it because I found it so charming at the time; years later I remembered it and combined its motif with a speckled background and a frilly border.

In this way, the fabrics at Tahoe blend strands of influence that discreetly reference the places I dreamed of visiting as a child.

3.
Вѣра
9.
17.
4.
6.
13.
5.
11.
1.
ДАМСК
Приложен
за
Узоры букетовъ, ги
выпуклой гладью, и
подушекъ, салфетокъ.
№ 9—2
Изданіе
Невс
СПБ Ли

Марія
10.
8.
18.
7.
15.
14.
19.
Елена
12.
2.
20
21.
ЬЛІЯ
ДАМЪ
выпиванія
кретона, для
П.Б.
22.

GOLFO DI
VENETIA
MARE
ADRIATICUM

FOLKLORIC JEWELRY

One of the great pleasures of living in New York City is discovering neighborhoods belonging to various diaspora. The East Village used to be home to Little Ukraine. The Ukrainian Museum was founded there in 1976 and exhibits the costumes of the country's many ethnic groups. I especially love the jewelry: many strands of coral or glass trade beads piled high, often with coins and ribbons. Most impressive are the giant woven collars of colorful, tiny "seed beads"—the very same that Europeans brought from Venice to the plains of North America. (These compact and easily transportable trade items also made their way across Russia and were incorporated into the costumes of many indigenous tribes of Siberia, replacing the shells and bones of earlier adornment.) The richness of materials and multiplicity of crafts on view in the museum reveal Ukraine as an important cultural crossroad.

As I developed a keen interest in folkloric decorative art, I began to collect jewelry from the places I have traveled to and that influence my work—Iran, Russia, and many former Soviet republics. Often I find pieces in America, as immigrants from the former Russian Empire brought over precious items and preserved them from war-ravaged twentieth-century Europe. Each piece feels personal, and imparts valuable information about the lifestyle and tastes of distant cultures.

Indeed, jewelry confers social prestige and expresses the aesthetics and sophistication of the person wearing it. It also acts as an open display of capital—never more so than in nomadic cultures, where it was one of the principal forms of wealth and readily convertible into currency. The Turkmen women of Central Asia wore lavish ornaments on their entire person. Aside from massive solid silver cuffs and headdresses encrusted with precious stones, silver items such as pendants, chains, and coins were sewn to their clothes and even attached to their braided hair. Travelers often described these tribal women as wearing armor; they were not far off, since a talismanic significance was attributed to these adornments—carnelian and turquoise were thought to possess protective properties. Moreover, the tinkling sound of the jewelry was considered magical.

PATCHWORK QUILTS

Appropriately, my link to quilts is a domestic, feminine one; my mother and my aunts are quite good quilters. It never occurred to me until recently that this was living American Folk art, perhaps because I had such a personal connection to it.

Despite its strong association with Americana, the art of the patchwork quilt—which involves both complex stitching and pattern making—is found around the world. In Europe it can be traced back at least to medieval times when quilts were mentioned in inventories as family heirlooms.

Early settlers from England and the Netherlands established quilting as a craft in North America, where it rapidly became a popular pastime for women. They often shared the work of making large bed covers. These quilting bees alleviated the hardship of the pioneering lifestyle and helped create a sense of community among a population that was often on the move.

There are so many reasons to love quilts. They have a nomadic lure. As bedding, they are practical objects that can be commemorative items or repositories of family history. They are also useful historical documents that preserve fragments of textile. But above all else, as they create new patterns out of disparate designs, quilts are a discreet visual form of poetic expression.

TURKEY RED

When I was first married I bought a length of red paisley cloth incorporating the Persian heraldic motif of the lion and the sun. This printed cotton was a standard Russian export item to Iran and a token of the global popularity of Turkey red. I made a pair of cushions but the fabric quickly frayed as it was so old. It was this disappointing attempt to add a Persian twist to my home that led me to the fabric mill in Alsace where I now produce my textiles.

Red is a popular color but until relatively recently it was difficult to produce a colorfast red dye. The story of this quest is an example of the circular motion of influence between East and West that underlies the history of the textile industry. Intense red required a lengthy and complex dying process using a pigment derived from the madder root. The recipe originated in Turkey or India. In the 1740s its secret was brought to France, where it was known as "rouge Andrinople," after the Turkish city now known as Edirne.

In the early nineteenth century a French chemist from Alsace created a synthetic formula and the manufacturing of Turkey red cottons boomed, spreading to mills in Manchester and Scotland, and eventually to the rest of the industrialized world. These bright cotton prints became one of the top export products of the nineteenth and twentieth centuries. Red entered the national dress of many countries as headscarves and shawls, or, in the case of America, bandanas.

The cushion on the wicker chair: Andrinople.

GREENWICH

CONNECTICUT HERITAGE

"Good decorating needs imperfection. It is the need to accommodate quirks and mix styles that stimulates creativity."

A house is alive. It comes with a past, not just in its architectural bones, but in the decorative choices of its former inhabitants. What I so love about the family house in Connecticut where I spent my teenage years is the haphazard mix of French and American styles. The previous owners had archetypal 1980s preppy taste. When my family moved from France, in came Empire furniture and other family heirlooms. The Greenwich green carpet was removed and the prep school stickers peeled from the windows, but old rose chintzes remained, as did a wonderful chinoiserie wallpaper in the dining room. Antiques from my mother's San Francisco family added a further layer of history to the house: lamps, oriental vases, quilts, sturdy furnishings, and lots of books.

The disorderly bookcases are the soul of the house. Upstairs on the children's floor (now grandchildren's floor), *Hardy Boys* stories and *The Three Musketeers* are stacked spine to spine beside my brother's science fiction collection. A mishmash of college textbooks is still present and often useful. Siblings and parents are represented together on these shelves, and it gives me great comfort to know that I can always rummage and find something interesting to read.

Under the surface of bourgeois tranquility and respect for objects, the Connecticut house is full of unexpected juxtapositions, and forms the perfect backdrop for adventures. As the eldest of four children I became a storyteller, the Wendy Darling of an eager and rambunctious gang. I created an underwater world, and then a mushroom world, each with their own languages and characters. My parents' garden was our flower shop, and acorn shells provided us with teacups. At times I remember hoping for a quiet corner where I could play undisturbed. My siblings taught me to be adaptive and flexible—qualities that were not innate, but proved to be quite necessary to the art of home decoration in accommodating the needs and tastes of others.

MAURICE DRUON
PLON

LE MOMENT DE LA REFLEXION.
A LITTLE TOUR IN FRANCE
HENRY JAMES
TOME V
TOME VI
TOME VII
LES ROIS MAUDITS I LE ROI DE FER
LES ROIS MAUDITS II LA REINE ÉTRANGLÉE
LES ROIS MAUDITS III LES POISONS DE LA COURONNE
LES ROIS MAUDITS IV LA LOI DES MÂLES
LES ROIS MAUDITS V LA LOUVE DE FRANCE
LES ROIS MAUDITS VI LE LIS ET LE LION
LES ROIS MAUDITS VII QUAND UN ROI PERD LA FRANCE
DE SÉVIGNÉ LETTRES 1
DE SÉVIGNÉ LETTRES 2
DE SÉVIGNÉ LETTRES 3
DE SÉVIGNÉ LETTRES 4
LETTRES 5
LETTRES 6
ŒUVRES
ŒUVRES
PLANTES

W 西
E 東
N 北
中
一 萬

A TURKMEN RUG

There was a time when the Turkmen rug was an indispensible element in a sophisticated décor. They were first imported via Russia for smoking rooms or studies, and hence were known as "Gentlemen's Carpets." The historical trajectory of a nomadic tribal rug to living rooms across Europe is of particular interest to me since the carpet in the photograph belonged to my French grandparents, and my husband has Turkmen ancestry. It is a link between East and West that is so ubiquitous it is easily overlooked.

Turkmen carpets have a simple geometry: Identical octagonal patterns are placed in rows on a plain red field (derived from the madder plant). In Europe the repeated motif is called "elephant's foot," while the Turkmen call it *gul*, from the Persian word for rose. Indeed, this motif is also described as a rosette. There is no conclusive theory on what it represents despite its centuries-old popularity all along the Silk Road, from China to Byzantium.

The strong link to the Silk Road explains the prominence of the Turkmen carpet in the Russian Orientalist style. At the height of the European scramble for colonies across the globe, the Russian Empire was expanding across Central Asia. The legendary cities of Tashkent, Bukhara, and Samarkand fell to Tsarist armies in the 1860s; Khiva in 1873. Tribal carpets started to flood their great bazaars, reaching Western markets at a time when a fascination with the Orient was all the rage. By 1898, the ancient Silk Road cities were linked to Russia by rail. This modern infrastructure led to export of carpets on an industrial scale, allowing them to make their way into homes throughout Europe.

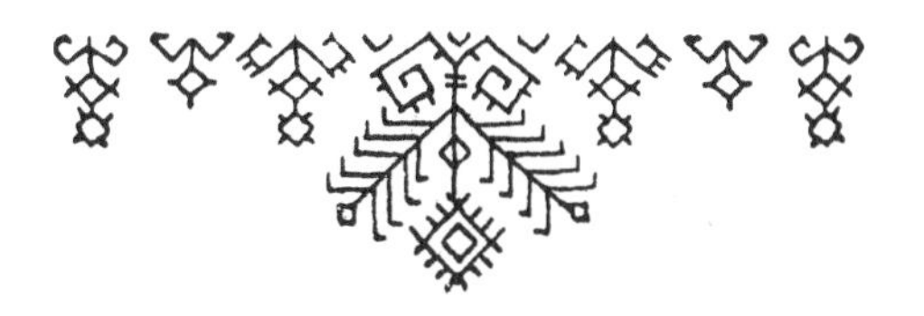

Табл. IV.

ТЕКИНСКІЕ ОРНАМЕНТЫ А. А. АСТАФЬЕВА. Собранные въ Ахалъ-Текинской экспедиціи

№21

№23

ХРОМОЛИТ. З. И. МАРКУСЪ С.ПЕТЕРБУРГЪ.

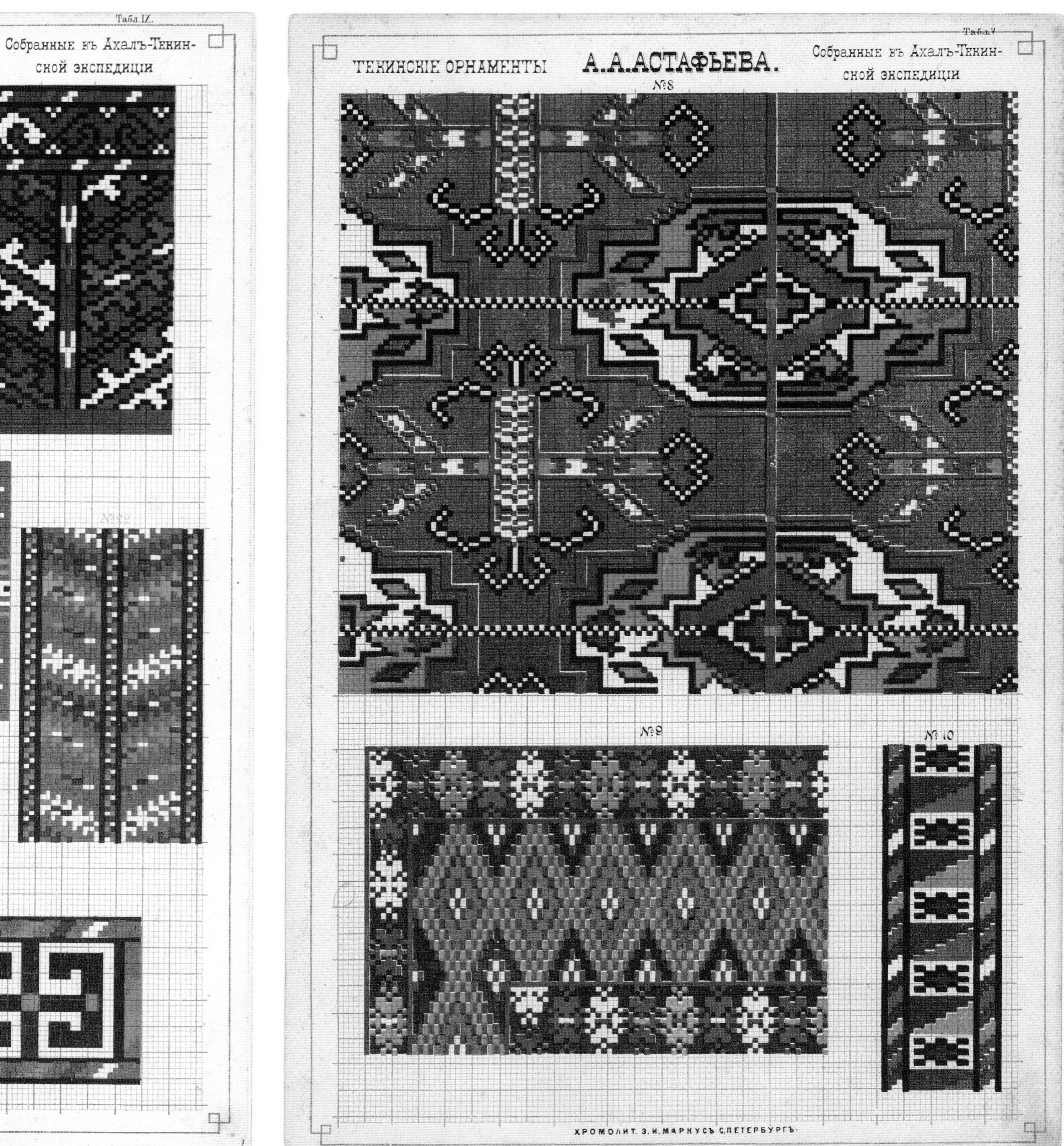

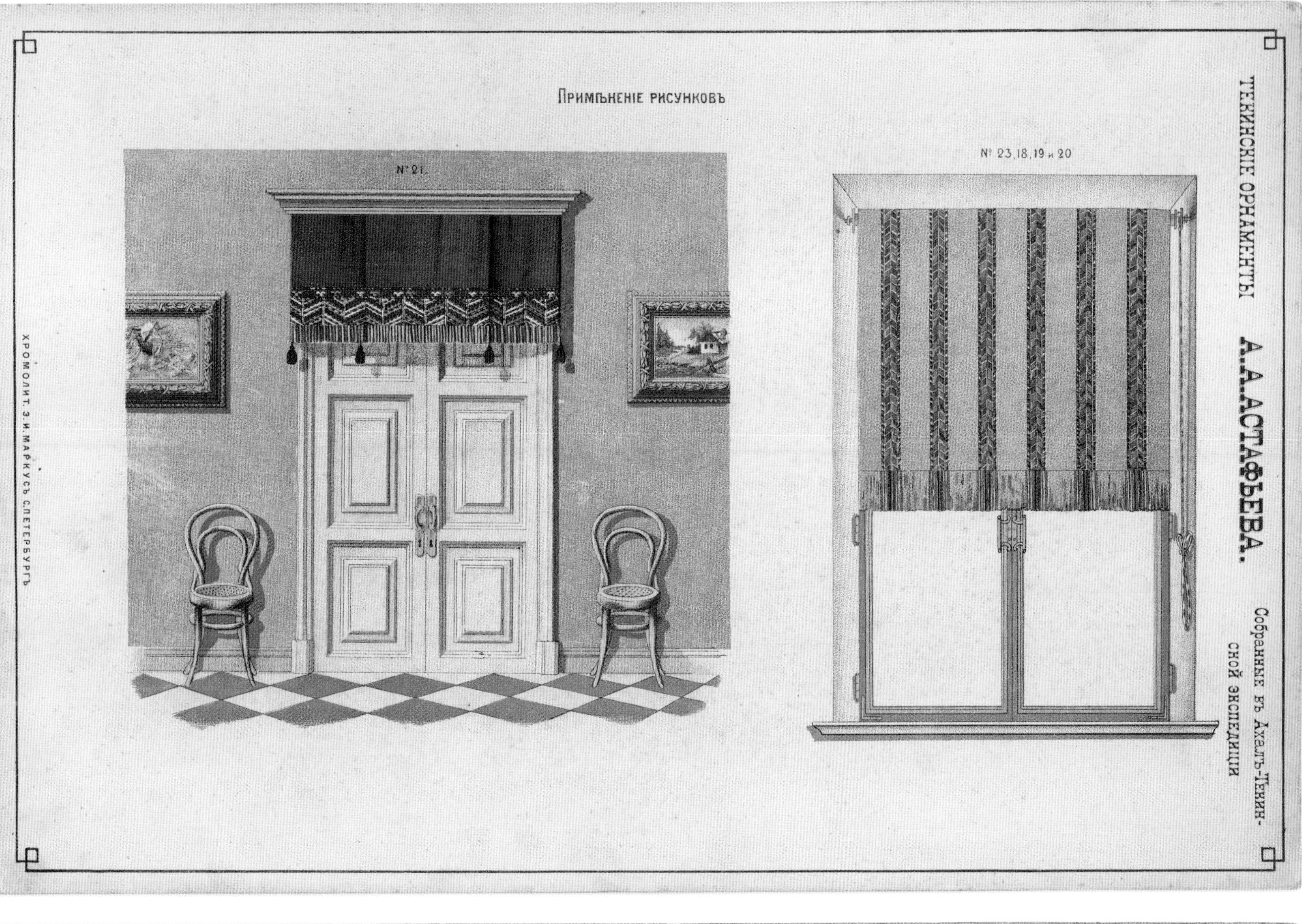
Примѣненіе рисунковъ
№ 21.
№ 23, 18, 19 и 20
ТЕКИНСКІЕ ОРНАМЕНТЫ
А.А.АСТАФЬЕВА.
Собранные въ Ахалъ-Текин-
ской экспедиціи
Хромолит. Э.И. Маркусъ С.Петербургъ

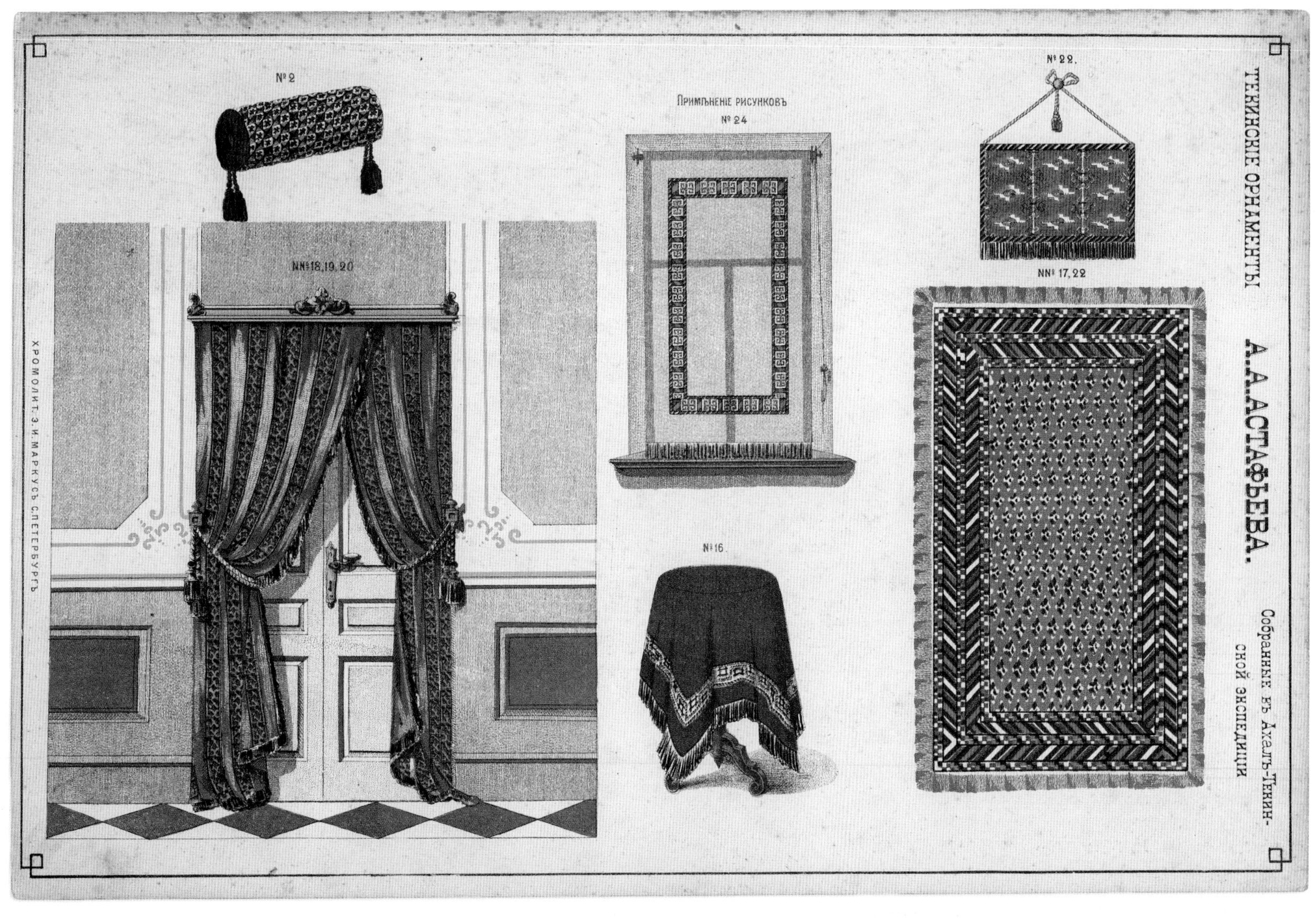
№ 2
Примѣненіе рисунковъ
№ 24
№ 22.
№№ 18, 19, 20
№№ 17, 22
№ 16.
ТЕКИНСКІЕ ОРНАМЕНТЫ
А.А.АСТАФЬЕВА.
Собранные въ Ахалъ-Текин-
ской экспедиціи
Хромолит. Э.И. Маркусъ С.Петербургъ

PAISLEY

Nothing exemplifies the power of textile design to spread around the world better than the story of paisley pattern. When it comes to fabrics, there are no borders. Beauty travels fast. Originally it was a Persian motif called *boteh*, or shrub. There is no consensus on what this shape represents. It could be a bent cypress tree or a flame, both sacred in Zoroastrianism, the ancient religion of Iran. Some see it as a pine cone. More prosaically, the Russians call it a cucumber. In India it is a mango, and in Britain it is sometimes referred to as a Welsh pear.

At the foot of the Himalayas, in the valley of Kashmir, the paisley motif started its journey toward becoming the first international fashion accessory. Sultan Zain-ul-Abidin, who ruled Kashmir in the fifteenth century, encouraged weavers from Persia and Central Asia to move to his kingdom. The region soon became known for its finely woven pashmina, embellished with borders of colored silk in floral paisleys, sometimes with gold and silver thread. These delicate shawls could take years to make. Mughal emperors and Persian Shahs wound them as sashes around their waists. Over time, and due to the expanding reach of European colonization, they became an indispensable accessory in both Eastern and Western courts.

Like all luxury items, the Kashmiri import was a victim of its own success. By the early nineteenth century industrial Europe had developed the technology—particularly the French Jacquard looms—to make copies that were within the reach of middle-class ladies. The design was so popular in Europe that it spurred the burgeoning textile printing industry. No longer woven, paisley patterns were available in lengths of printed wool or cotton for dresses. As the nineteenth century progressed, the design became commonplace, gradually used for cheaper goods associated with peasant costumes, such as scarves. Hence the term "paisley" in English; it is actually a town in Scotland where mills manufactured woven shawls with such efficiency that they gave the motif its name.

UZBEK PLATES

The further from a cultural center, the wilder patterns become. The expansion of Russian colonial power to the East, across the steppes of Central Asia, meant that porcelain made for the Eastern market was traveling thousands of miles through forests and deserts to reach the great cities of the Silk Road.

I first encountered Russian export china when my husband and I looked for items made for the Persian market: blue-and-white teapots or plates with a central medallion containing portraits of Shahs from the Qajar dynasty. I soon fell in love with the strange baroque-oriental appeal of Central Asian porcelain. Despite a somewhat crude execution, Russian-made china (mainly plates and bowls used for plov and soups) was a luxury item for both city-dwellers and nomads. In the houses and palaces of Bukhara, for example, the porcelain was displayed in intricately carved and painted wall recesses—often the main form of domestic decoration alongside rugs and wall hangings. The nomadic tribes took equal pride in these items and constructed special traveling boxes to carry them safely along the steppes, across long distances and rugged terrain.

The story of porcelain production for Central Asia is very similar to that of textile production. Both industries originated with the need to provide European-style luxury goods such as Meissen china or French calico for the Russian elite. Soon, a new national style in porcelain and fabrics evolved, adapting to local taste and customs *au goût russe*. In my view, however, this Russian production was never as compelling and creative as when it merged with the Central Asian love of pattern.

There are two main categories of Central Asian porcelain: Gardner and Kuznetsov. In the late nineteenth century the Gardner factory produced bowls and tea sets, painted with delicate flower sprays in blue or pink. During the twentieth century the Kuznetsov factory (which had absorbed Gardner) mass-produced plates in the local taste, with bright, festive decorative motifs. These plates have a more ethnic feel to them, reflecting awakening nationalism. Many are adorned with the cotton bolls so important to the local economy. Others have ikat patterns or tendriled florals.

THE PEASANT BLOUSE

Traditional peasant clothing has a long history of inspiring city chic with ancient designs reproduced in silk instead of coarse home-spun linen. In Russia, for example, a type of "couture" folk costume was very fashionable in the late nineteenth century. The cut resembled a long Victorian dress, which was then embellished with lace from the northern Vologda region, strips of colorful ribbon, and cross-stitch embroidery. The workmanship was sophisticated but the motifs were essentially composite and not representative of any regional culture. These beautiful dresses are well documented—turn-of-the-century ladies often wore them in photographic portraits. One can surmise they were expensive and possibly even "fashion forward," as there are images of the avant-garde artist Natalia Goncharova posing in this peasant style.

Indeed, all over Eastern Europe at the time it was popular to express an appreciation of one's cultural heritage by wearing similar items. Nobody wore traditional dress with more panache than Queen Marie of Romania. She adopted the Romanian peasant blouse as her signature style, often wearing it with big studded leather belts, turbans, embroidered veils, and always with pearls. A granddaughter of Queen Victoria, she was only seventeen when she moved to Romania for her marriage to Ferdinand von Hohenzollern, who would rule Romania from 1914 to 1927.

Although it was not uncommon in her time for European royalty to display a fondness for picturesque national dress (one need look no further than her grandparents Queen Victoria and Prince Albert in Scottish garb), Queen Marie of Romania displayed an appreciation for the peasant art of her adoptive land that went beyond a sense of duty. She saw the beauty and timelessness of the Romanian peasant blouse and made it an item of high style. It would later inspire Yves Saint Laurent and many other designers in his wake.

Журавль и цапля
Медведь

ITALO CALVINO
DIFFICULT LOVES
Peace to End All
ENGLISH LITERATURE
WE ARE NO GROWN-UPS
THE PROTESTANT ETHIC AND THE SPIRIT OF CAPITALISM
Max Weber
Joan Didion
THE ART OF HAPPINESS
ALBERT CAMUS
Le premier homme
MONDE
SOPHIE
A Cambodian Prison Portrait Vann Nath
SHAH OF SHAHS
RYSZARD KAPUSCINSKI
PEYOTE
Buddhism
After AUSCHWITZ
LITERARY THEORY
JULIA CHILD
MY LIFE IN FRANCE
LAROUSSE
CHINESE
JOHN BERGER WAYS OF SEEING
The Magic Pudding
NORMAN LINDSAY
SPECIAL MICKEY GEANT

FAIRY TALES

I trace my first aesthetic encounter with Russia to the illustrated fairy tales of Ivan Bilibin, which I read as a child in the widely available Père Castor edition. In nineteenth-century Russia, the field of children's literature was largely non-existent. Instead, the nation's youth was mostly fed British poetry and German fairy tales. Bilibin championed the rediscovery of Russia's oral fairy tales and believed that they should be illustrated in a realistic manner, one that accurately depicted the ethnographic details found in printed cloths, embroideries, woodcarvings, and icons. To this end he undertook two field expeditions to the Russian North, in 1902 and in 1904, in order to gather folk art and photograph architecture and paintings.

The richness of folk tradition in the Russian North would leave a lasting impression on him, as it did on the painter Wassily Kandinsky, who had made a similar ethnographic expedition a decade earlier. Kandinsky would write in his diary: "I still remember the first time I stepped inside the rooms of an isba. I stopped dead in my tracks, astonished before the amazing paintings that surrounded me on all sides. The table, the benches, the great oven, important in Russian peasant houses, the wardrobes and every object were painted with bright-colored, large-figured decorations. I found myself surrounded on all sides by painting, into which I had thus penetrated."

Bilibin was equally enraptured by the colors and patterns he saw. But whereas Kandinsky turned to abstraction to capture the spirit of his experience, Bilibin strove to record the designs with minute historical precision. Mixing fantasy and historical authenticity, Bilibin succeeded in creating a magical world that would grip generations of children. His books now also provide invaluable documentary evidence for those interested in Russian motifs. I have been able to identify textiles in his drawings as those now held in museums. I once matched a wooden printing block with one of his patterns and decided to make it into a fabric again, appropriately named after him.

Журавль и
Медвѣдь
Рисунки
Изданіе
Москва
1907
Сказка

мнимою Еленою Прекрасною, то царь вельми возрадовался въ сердцѣ своемъ, что получилъ такое сокровище, котораго онъ давно желалъ; а коня златогриваго вручилъ Ивану-царевичу. Иванъ-царевичъ сѣлъ на того коня и выѣхалъ за городъ, посадилъ съ собою Елену Прекрасную и поѣхалъ, держа путь къ государству царя Долмата. Сѣрой же волкъ живетъ у царя Афрона день, другой и третій, вмѣсто прекрасной королевны Елены, а на четвертый день пришелъ къ царю Афрону проситься въ чистомъ полѣ погулять, чтобъ разбить тоску-печаль лютую. Какъ возговорилъ ему царь Афронъ: „Ахъ, прекрасная моя королевна Елена! я для тебя все сдѣлаю“. И тотчасъ приказалъ нянюшкамъ и мамушкамъ и всѣмъ придворнымъ боярынямъ съ прекрасною королевною идти въ чистое поле гулять.

Иванъ же царевичъ ѣхалъ путемъ-дорогою съ Еленою Прекрасною, разговаривалъ съ нею и забылъ было про сѣраго волка; да потомъ вспомнилъ: „Ахъ, гдѣ-то мой сѣрой волкъ“? Вдругъ откуда ни взялся — сталъ онъ передъ Иваномъ-царевичемъ и сказалъ ему: „Садись, Иванъ-царевичъ, на меня, на сѣраго волка, а прекрасная королевна пусть ѣдетъ на конѣ златогривомъ“. Иванъ-царевичъ сѣлъ на сѣраго волка, и поѣхали они въ государство царя Долмата. Ѣхали они долго ли, коротко ли, и, доѣхавъ до того государства, за три версты отъ города остановились. Иванъ-царевичъ началъ просить сѣраго волка: „Слушай ты, другъ мой любезной, сѣрой волкъ! сослужилъ ты мнѣ много службъ, — сослужи мнѣ и послѣднюю: не можешь ли ты оборотиться въ коня златогриваго на мѣсто этого, потому что съ этимъ златогривымъ конемъ мнѣ разстаться не хочется“.

The Brothers Karamazov

L'ISLAM
ET LES
MUSULMANS

LONDON

A HOUSE FOR ALL SEASONS

When my children Alexander and Rose were only just toddlers my husband and I decided to relocate to London, where we had friends and family. This allowed me to travel more frequently to France for my textile production, but also to widen my cultural horizon as I discovered the countries of Eastern Europe and Central Asia. Traveling is a way to keep thinking about design and pattern; I am always interested to see how cultures overlap and influences are blended and reconfigured.

This mixing of all the things I love is the hallmark of the London house. It is an early Georgian building, full of charm and short on space. For this reason the décor is deliberately old-fashioned and cozy, with upholstered walls and knick-knacks just about everywhere—a very Proustian sense of voluptuousness. I put a lot of effort into sourcing light fixtures and picture frames. My taste is quite consistent, I love carved and painted wood, icons, Caucasian rugs, nineteenth-century furniture from Sweden and Russia, French lamps, antique frames and, of course, lots of pillows.

"The expression of personality in a house has always been an interest of mine and when I travel I prefer to visit homes rather than museums."

Since home is a personal space, it should be filled with photographs and objects of sentimental value. These objects, as they are positioned around the house, create a silent dialog. I tend to group items that are alike. This creates a sense of narrative and continuity. At the same time I try to retain an element of surprise, even of incongruity. Every now and again I will mix things up: for example I recently moved all the icons from the living room to the bedroom.

At certain times of year, the house gets dressed up. Tablecloths change with the seasons. Painted eggs and flowers are displayed in the spring for Easter and the Persian New Year, Nauruz. The house is never more festive than during the lead up to Christmas when it is festooned with wintergreens and tinsel. More than any other space, London changes to the rhythms of my pursuits. It is both a laboratory of decorating ideas and a self-portrait.

Charmed Lives in Greece

POLO

A DASH OF CASTAING

Until I walked into the Madeleine Castaing store on the corner of Rue Bonaparte and Rue Jacob in Paris I hadn't fully understood that interior decoration could be so imaginative and personal. I was a student in my early twenties, and Castaing, who had lived above her antique shop, had just passed away. Her boutique was still run as a salon for devotees by her loyal factotum, Mme Lombardini, who needed to be coaxed into giving prices, as, on any given day, items were not necessarily for sale. It was a warren of low-ceilinged rooms, each decorated as a whimsical stage set for an unorthodox mix of furniture styles—Napoleon III, Regency, and Biedermeier—displayed alongside needlepoint rugs, plaster busts, and other knick-knacks. The effect was an elusive sense of familiarity, like entering into a favorite nineteenth-century novel.

A member of the Montparnasse set between the wars, Madeleine Castaing had been a close friend of artists such as Blaise Cendrars, Erik Satie, Jean Cocteau, and Chaïm Soutine. "I decorate houses the way others paint pictures or write books," she explained, and her interiors reflected erudition, confidence, and originality. Like the other post-war decorators—Emilio Terry, Georges Geoffroy, Victor Grandpierre, Maison Jensen—her style was a nostalgic reinvention of the charm and soothing domesticity of the dream childhood country house of French life before the two deadly twentieth-century wars. It was also free from rules of any kind. This is why the line of fabrics and carpets she re-edited and used in many of her interiors has a timelessness to it. All houses can use a little dash of Castaing fairy dust.

Terracotta torso of a sailor: From the sitting room of Castaing's house in Lèves.

THE TRUST
LIEBLING

INTERIOR WATERCOLORS

Any serious student of interiors has to start by looking through albums of nineteeth-century watercolor renderings of rooms. Not only are they completely magical and transporting, but they can be considered an early form of interior publication. Indeed, despite chronicling the palaces of the aristocracy in European capital cities such as Paris, St. Petersburg, Naples, or Vienna, they coincide with the birth of popular interior design and decoration among the bourgeois class. Pride of place is given to wallpapers, carpets, and textiles, all now industrially produced—the Empire and Biedermeier styles declined in multiple colorways and adapted to all seasons. The books of Charlotte Gere, Stephen Calloway, Peter Thornton, and the great Mario Praz, are all essential reading. There are many other little gems such as the works of Mary Ellen Best.

The last great artist in this tradition of interior portraiture is undoubtedly Alexandre Sérébriakoff. Born into a gifted family of artists in prerevolutionary St. Petersburg (his mother's uncle was Alexandre Benois of Ballets Russes fame), he was forced to emigrate to Paris in 1925. He became a great lover of his adopted city. In hundreds of meticulous little sketches he recorded the streets and buildings of post-war Paris.

From the 1940s through to the 1980s Sérébriakoff worked for the who's who of aesthetic high society —John Fowler, the Windsors, Chanel, the Rothschilds family, Christian Bérard, and many others. He is perhaps best known for documenting every room in Charles de Beistegui's legendary Château de Groussay. These watercolors are included in the introduction to the Sotheby's catalog of the 1999 Groussay sale. It was my first encounter with Sérébriakoff.

The interiors I prefer are those he made for other Russian émigrés. His attention to detail and charming rendering is suffused with nostalgia. The owner of this little apartment in Neuilly was Sophia Dragomirova Lukomskaya, a friend of his mother's who had posed in her youth for the most famous portrait painters in Russia, Ilya Repin and Valentin Serov.

СЕРОВЪ
KIEV

EDGE OF EMPIRE
THE ORIENTALIST
The Sultans of Paradise
Venise a l'Orient
INSIDE VENICE
Dumas
Temples of Ancient Egypt
A SHORT HISTORY OF BYZANTIUM

Francis Robinson
VOLUME I BOOKS
CYRUS GHANI
MAGE
The Dynamics of the Iranian Revolution
SUNY
LES ROIS OUBLIÉS
PRAEGER
A Guide to the Contents of the Qur'an
Ithaca Press
KHODADAD FARMANFARMAIAN
THE ISLAMIC ENLIGHTENMENT
The modern struggle between faith and reason
CHRISTOPHER DE BELLAIGUE
A Matter of Survival
Kadivar
Farewell Shiraz
An Iranian Memoir of Revolution and Exile
AUC PRESS
The Palace of Darius at Susa
The Great Royal Residence of Achaemenid Persia
TOM HOLLAND
PERSIAN FIRE
SANDRA MACKEY
THE IRANIANS
The Heritage of Persia
FRYE
از تهران
تا کاراکاس
نفت و سیاست
در ایران
منوچهر فرمانفرمائیان
CURZON'S PERSIA
PERSIA
HON. G. CURZON M.P.
VOL. I.
VOL. II.
LONGMANS & Co
A HISTORY OF PERSIA
LIEUT-COL. P. M. SYKES
VOL. II
VOL. I
MACMILLAN & Co
THE ADVENTURES OF HAJJI BABA OF ISPAHAN
ANDRÉ PARROT
OLIVER WATSON

SPIRITUALITY IN THE LAND OF THE NO
MICHAEL AXWORTHY IRAN: EMPIRE OF
TWELVE DAYS IN PERSIA
AGE OF HAFEZ
TRAVELS IN PERS
THE AURA O
JOHN SIMPSON &
MARTIN LINGS
THE ASSASSIN LEGENDS
FARHAD DAFTARY
DESMOND HARNEY
Life of the Ayatollah
Baqer Moin
THE GOLDEN AGE OF PERSIA
RICHARD N. FRYE
NATIONALIZATION AND ITS AFTERMATH
ineveh to New York
Lily Izadi Monadjemi
PARSI LOSING AN ENEMY
Yale
ABBAS AMANAT IRAN A MODERN HISTORY
The Sense of Unity
Chicago
STEMPEL
Inside the Iranian Revolution
Indiana
Debacle: The American Failure in Iran
Ledeen & Lewis
KNOPF
Persia: An Archaeological Guide
Sylvia A. Matheson
FABER
THE GREAT AMERICAN PLUNDER OF PERSIA'S ANTIQUITIES
PERSIA IN WORLD WAR I AND ITS CONQUEST BY GREAT BRITAIN
EARTHLY PARADISES
Mysticism and Dissent
دیوان حافظ
HISTOIRE DE L'EMPIRE PERSE
Fayard
ANDRÉ GODARD
THE ART OF IRAN
PRAEGER
IRAN and the Rise of REZA SHAH
From Qajar Collapse to Pahlavi Power
CYRUS GHANI
I.B.Tauris
ETERNAL IRAN
ISLAMIC TILES
Venetia Porter
Persian Mythology
JOHN R HINNELLS
QAJAR STUDIES
Qajar Studies
Entertainment in Qajar Persia
SELECTED WORKS
15 centimes
Le Rire
JOURNAL HUMORISTIQUE PARAISSANT LE SAMEDI
LE MUSÉE DES SOUVERAINS
S. M. MOUZAFFER-ED-DINE, SHAH DE PERSE
SIMS
VOLUME III
ISLAMIC PERIOD

S.ŻUKOWSKI 1928

RUSSIAN EMBROIDERY

The embroideries that I frame and display in my dining room were all originally part of the vast collection of domestic textiles and festive costumes assembled by the visionary Natalia de Shabelsky (1841–1905), who devoted her life to the conservation of Russian folk traditions. As a young bride, Shabelsky began to study and collect the work of the women on her husband's estate in Ukraine, ultimately establishing a school for embroidery there. She was soon fascinated by the variety of color and pattern and, more importantly, intrigued by the meaning of the ancient symbols preserved from remotest times and perpetuated in the beautiful embroidery of ritual cloths.

This research became her passion. Shabelsky traveled throughout Russia collecting fine textiles and other folk objects, eventually creating a museum in her Moscow home which housed over 4,000 pieces. She also took her collection around the world, including to the World's Fair in Chicago in 1893 and to Paris in 1900. As the world marveled at new feats in steel engineering, Shabelsky shared a connection to an ancient past.

It would be anachronistic to call Natalia de Shabelsky a feminist, but she preserved essential evidence of the importance of women and their work. Whether they related to fertility rituals or cult worship, the visual motifs embroidered by village women in Russia—goddesses with upraised arms, trees, birds, sun disks, horses—had a particular significance, somewhat muted and lost in time, but one that retained a spiritual, quasi-talismanic function.

Shabelsky moved to Paris in 1902 and died in France shortly thereafter. Her collection was sold and dispersed to collectors but the bulk was thankfully transferred to the Russian Museum of Ethnography in St. Petersburg. Another significant portion of Shabelsky's collection entered the Brooklyn Museum holdings and is searchable online on the Metropolitan Museum of Art's website, where it provides a valuable archive for artists and designers.

1.

2.

3.

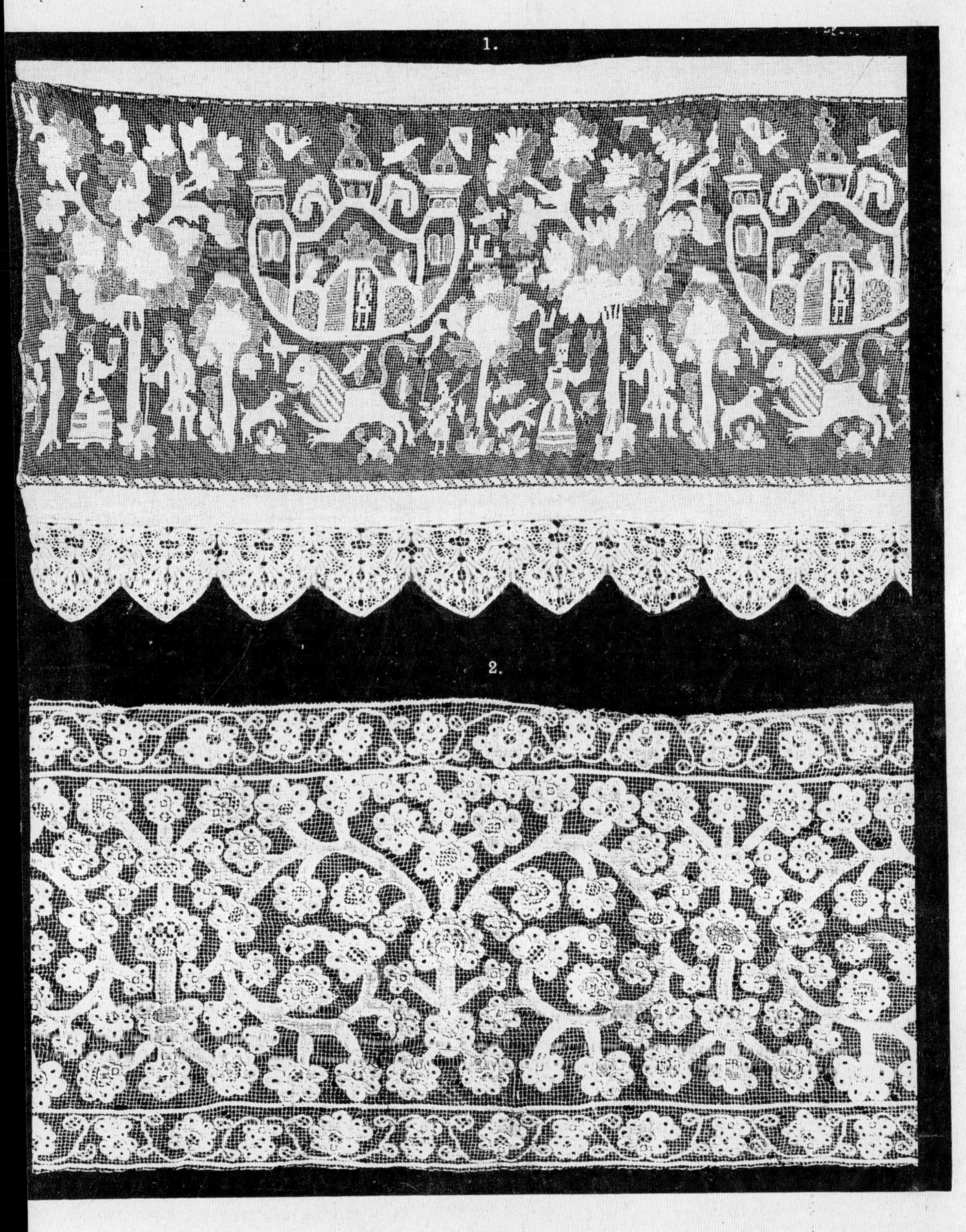
1.
2.

The Essential Turgenev
Turgenev
Northwestern University Press

Cer:
Soufré

E. H. CARR THE ROMANTIC EXILES
Isaiah Berlin RUSSIAN THINKERS
SISTERS SINAI
GRAHAM ALLCOTT
Patrick Boucheron

Hope Against Hope
The Writing of Art
DONTS FOR HUSBANDS
BREAD AND ASHES
RUSSIAN COLONIAL SOCIETY IN TASHKENT, 1865–1923
Mihail Sebastian For Two Thousand Years
Music's Modern Muse
Frankenstein · Mary Shelley
Comrade Baron
LOST KINGDOM
JAMIL AHMAD The Wandering Falcon
Peter Matthiessen THE SNOW LEOPARD
The English Eccentrics Edith Sitwell
CAUCASUS
DAPHNE du MAURIER · REBECCA
PATRICK LEIGH FERMOR
THE OREGON TRAIL
E.H. CARR THE ROMANTIC EXILES
RUSSIAN THINKERS
WITTGENSTEIN'S FAMILY LETTERS
BRIAN McGUINNESS
PETER WINSLOW
MARK TWAIN'S SAN FRANCISCO
THE HERO WITH A THOUSAND FACES
The Love of Strangers
A SCREEN OF TIME
SYMPATHIZER
THE GREAT TERROR STALIN'S PURGE OF THE THIRTIES
GREEN ON BLUE
THE AGE OF GOLD
H.W. BRANDS

JOHN le CARRÉ
A Legacy of Spies

Mr T.E.J. Nolan's
Manor House
20
17

DAUGHTER OF PERSIA

1921.
ЖАРЪ ПТИЦА.
„JAR-PTITZA"
RUSSISCHE MONATSSCHRIFT
FÜR KUNST-LITERATUR
REVUE RUSSE D'ART
ET DE LITERATURE

ЖАРЪ-ПТИЦА
JAR-PTITZA
№14
1926
J.Bilibine
И.Б.
1926

ЖАРЪ ПТИЦА
№10 JAR-PTITZA 1923

JAR
PTITZA
ЖАРЪ
ПТИЦА
№12

ЖАРЪ ПТИЦА
№8 JAR-PTITZA 1922

SOVIET GRAPHIC ART

I am willing to buy books for their covers. The paper, the typeface, the choice in binding—even before it is opened a book is the ultimate object of seduction. My interest in graphic art runs parallel to my love of fabrics. The industrialization of printing in both industries allowed design to reach wider markets and resulted in a great flowering of talent. At the turn of the century, all great European cities were home to a surge in publishing, advertising, and poster art. St. Petersburg, in particular, witnessed an explosion of creativity from the late nineteenth century through to the Stalinist terror of the 1930s. These years mark a triumph of Russian art in all spheres. It was national and international, and always avant-garde.

The career of one of Russia's most successful book illustrators, Sergei Chekhonin, spans these turbulent decades of war and revolution. Like many aspiring artists of his generation, he was influenced by Sergei Diaghilev's journal, *World of Art*, and the innovative graphic work of its contributors Léon Bakst, Ivan Bilibin, Alexandre Benois, and Konstantin Somov. In their wake, Chekhonin created innovative and playful typefaces, borders, and vignettes that blended art nouveau and traditional folk elements.

Chekhonin found his life upended by the revolution and the resulting economic chaos. Already socially engaged, he organized a council to address the problems and goals of the industrial arts. He was consequently appointed first artistic director of the State Porcelain Factory, where his skill with the pen allowed him to bridge the old and the new. With bold contrasting colors and geometric abstraction he pioneered the use of propaganda on porcelain. Beautifully inscribed around his plates, among flowers and garlands, are didactic slogans such as: *He who is not with us is against us; Struggle gives birth to heroes; The kingdom of workers and peasants shall have no end.*

In the early 1920s Chekhonin also collaborated on *Zhar-Ptitsa*, the most famous of the post-revolutionary Russian art journals. He was commissioned to design its first cover. It features a big red rose, which I loved so much I designed my daughter's room around it. Chekhonin left the Soviet Union permanently in 1928 and emigrated to Paris, home to many of the artists associated with Diaghilev's Ballets Russes.

THE LIFE OF A WARDROBE

As a house changes through the seasons, so do the colors, patterns, and materials that can be found in a closet. In the winter months I tend towards mohair, flowery or folkloric silks, velvet, and items with shine. In the summer it's all about cotton prints. A wardrobe is an interesting study since it is where fabrics are most alive.

I have collected beloved vintage items over the years and when I reshuffle them back into my closet when the weather changes, it is like seeing old friends again. They tend to all be French, perhaps because I spent my childhood in Paris. I have a predilection for Yves Saint Laurent from the 1970s and early 1980s. The quality of the prints is almost impossible to find today. Saint Laurent's vision of elegance was literary and exotic with a sense of bohemian cool. Despite being open to influences from all around the world, his use of color retained a certain Frenchness that makes his distinct East-West alchemy so successful. His personal favorite was his 1976 collection inspired by Russia, which drew on tsarist Russia and Léon Bakst's drawings for the Ballets Russes. Accented with a dramatic use of scarves, capes, and fur hats, the result was Orientalism squared. Nonetheless, this collection is still wearable today. In his own words, "Fashions fade, style is eternal."

I credit the Foundation YSL, established by Pierre Bergé in Paris in 2002, for introducing me to such rich fashion traditions from around the world: Indian robes, Moroccan caftans, Berber jewelry and, last but not least, traditional Russian clothing.

Alongside vintage fashion, I like to add authentic ethnic items to my wardrobe, such as an embroidered blouse from Romania or a Persian Qajar jacket. As I look for antique textiles, it is hard to resist an item I can actually wear. I am moved by the individual inventiveness of traditional costumes. They are festive and unpretentious, which makes them surprisingly contemporary.

FABRICS

“I wanted to travel back in time to the Silk Road and look for fabrics in the bazaars. My work is a mix of fantasy and historical authenticity.”

SWATCH BOOK

Throughout these pages, readers already familiar with my Décors Barbares fabrics may have recognized some of them, from the bedroom walls in Greenwich to the wickerware in Tahoe. They look best when they are not flat, but in motion, upholstered on a chair or in curtain folds. Textiles are three-dimensional. When I design fabrics I pin them up in different corners of my room to see how the patterns change with the light. I study them through squinted eyes to make sure the overall effect is always comforting, with no sharp shapes appearing in the shadows.

Very few of the fabrics match per se, but the colors all work together. This is what unifies the line, a Russian palette in the middle ground between joyfully bold and not too new. I drape works in progress next to existing designs; again, I move them around the room to test if they fit the atmosphere. The process is very organic and I have learned not to rush. I know the colors of a new fabric are finalized when I am excited to use it. The aim is to develop a product that is timeless and feels like it was always in the room.

Deciding which new fabric idea to pursue is the biggest challenge. I have a long list of possibilities, but the need to exercise restraint helps temper fleeting enthusiasm. My mind is full of imaginary spaces, often based on old photographs or paintings and many inspired by the places I visited as a child. If I still want to see a fabric a year after first visualizing it, I seriously consider starting the process of production.

In this sense, the collection should work like a well-curated closet—each time you open the doors, the clothes inside should offer a combination of options within a well-defined style to make dressing easy. Both in fashion and interior design, some prints carry a look while others are accents. My fabrics fall in both categories, with the purpose of enhancing decorating options. Following are a few of my designs in no particular order.

Curtain: Feuilles Nina. Chair: Aurel, original.

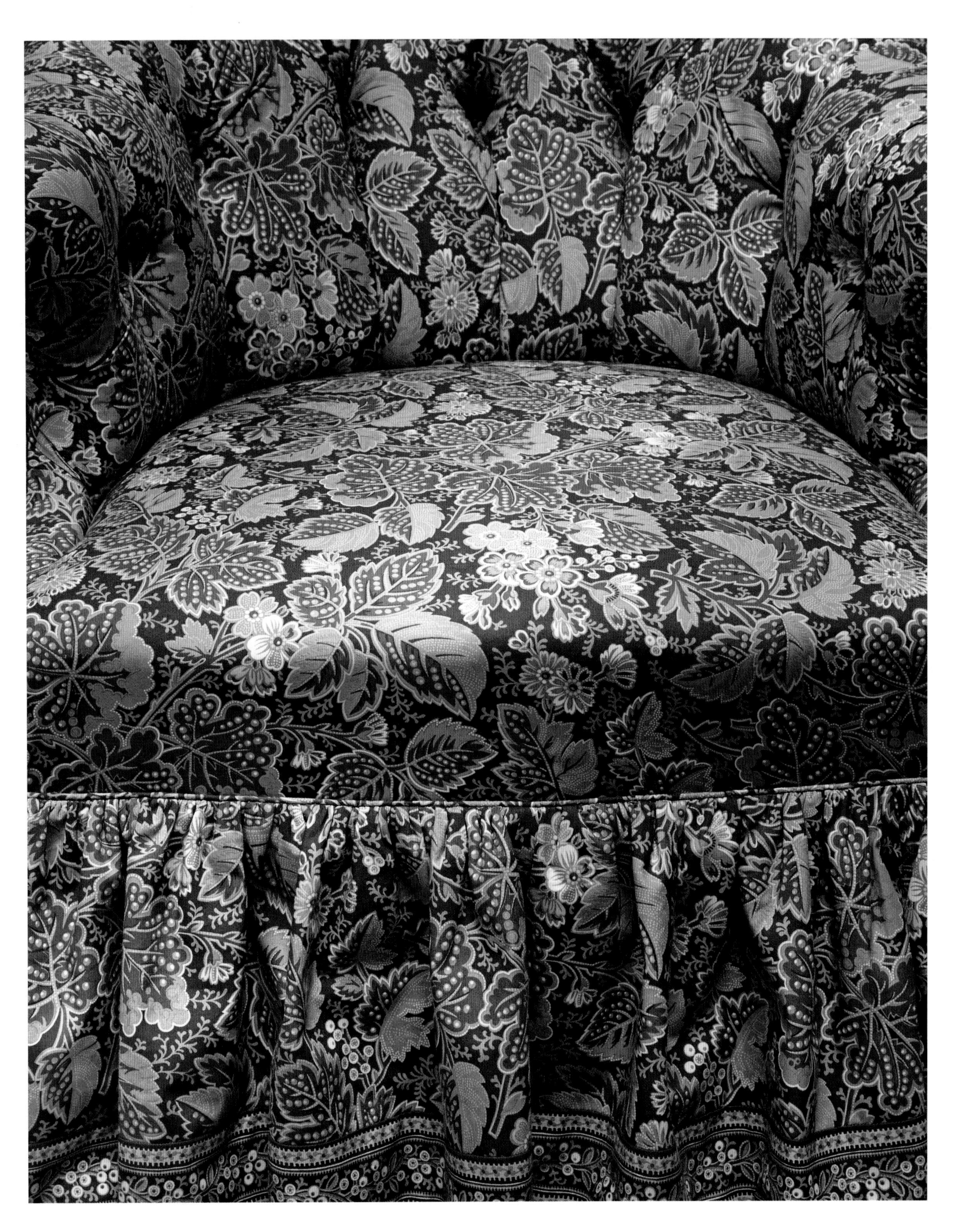

Above: Dans la Forêt, green. Opposite, clockwise from top left: Fleur de Steppes, red; Bilibine, red; Sadko, pink; Polonaise, red.

Above: Sarafane, indigo. Opposite, clockwise from top left: Les Groseilles, red and blue; Varykino; Casse-Noisette, pink; Natacha, beige.

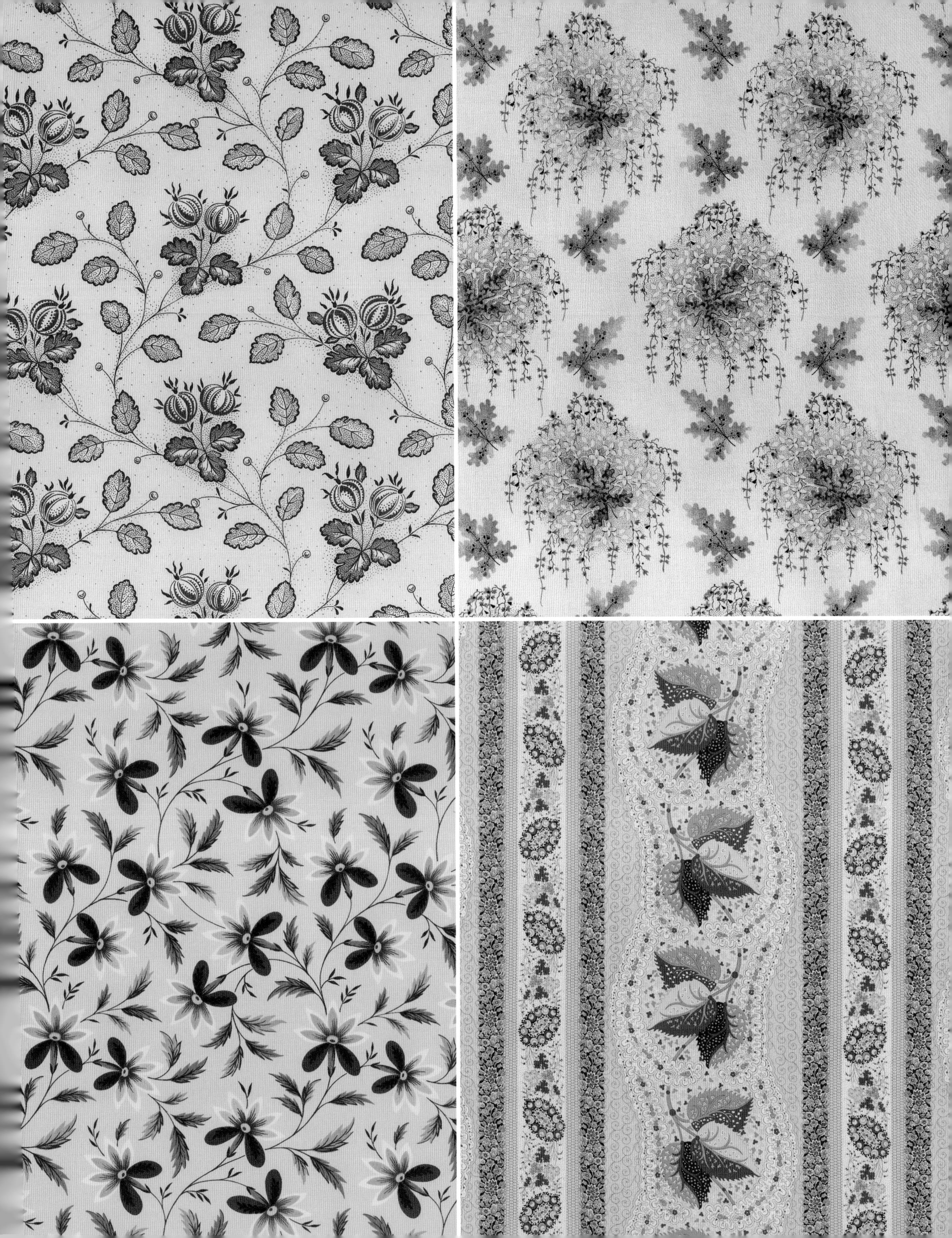

Above: Naboika, indigo. Opposite, clockwise from top left: Zénaide, original; Moujik; Rayures Datcha, red and blue; Véra, blue.

ACKNOWLEDGMENTS

This book is dedicated to my late sister Juliette, who was taken from us in the bloom of her life. Our shared memories of childhood led to a shared aesthetic vision which was invaluable to me in my decorative work. Above all, she was my greatest supporter; I would never have launched Décors Barbares without her unswerving conviction that my voice needed to be heard. I want to thank the rest of family, my mother, my brother Eric and his wife Emma, as well as my sister Marianne and her husband Alessandro, for stepping into Juliette's shoes and allowing me to decorate our family homes with Silk Road flourish.

My husband, Amir, and my children, Alexander and Rose, are well accustomed to having me *barbarify* their spaces without prior consultation. They have learned to live with appearing and disappearing objects, rickety chairs, furniture rearrangements ahead of shoots, and many more surprises my fabric design always has in store for them. I thank them for their patience and love.

Beatrice Vincenzini, my wonderful editor at Vendome, believed in this project from the start and gave me the purpose I needed when she suggested this book could be a tribute to my sister.

There would have been no book without Miguel Flores-Vianna's magic behind the camera as well as his friendship and guidance. I am equally indebted to Mary Robbins, who accompanied me on this journey from beginning to end—many thanks for your sanity and good humor. Thanks also to Brett Wood. How lucky to have work be such fun.

I want to thank David Netto for the marvelous foreword and the many years of friendship. Markham Roberts and James Sansum, the best of friends, were there every step of the way. Silk Rittson-Thomas provided me with all the beautiful flowers in London and with much encouragement besides.

I would also like to acknowledge, with much gratitude, the help and support of Lydie Greco, Andrew Steel, Sam Schats, Carol Kelly, Heather Nelson, Jean-Paul and Monique Tisseyre, Dan and Coleen Alley, Jean-Michel and Sandrine Borin, Laurence Stoeltzlen, and Dianne Gamarra.

Last but not least, a big thank you to all the team at Vendome: Mark Magowan, Francesco Venturi, David Shannon, Alexandra Black and Roger Barnard.

First published in 2020 by **The Vendome Press**
Vendome is a registered trademark of The Vendome Press, LLC

www.vendomepress.com

NEW YORK
Suite 2043,
244 Fifth Avenue,
New York, NY 10011

LONDON
63 Edith Grove,
London,
SW10 0LB

PUBLISHERS
Beatrice Vincenzini, Mark Magowan & Francesco Venturi

Distributed in North America by Abrams Books
Distributed in the UK, and rest of the world, by Thames & Hudson

ISBN: 978-0-86565-389-4

EDITOR Alexandra Black
PRODUCTION DIRECTOR Jim Spivey
DESIGNER Roger Barnard

Library of Congress Cataloging-in-Publication Data
Names: Farman-Farma, Nathalie, author. | Flores-Vianna, Miguel, photographer (expression)
Title: Décors barbares : the enchanting interiors of Nathalie Farman-Farma.
Description: New York : Vendome, 2020.
Identifiers: LCCN 2020021850 | ISBN 9780865653894 (hardcover)
Subjects: LCSH: Farman Farma, Nathalie--Themes, motives. | Textile fabrics in interior decoration.
| Ethnic art in interior decoration.
Classification: LCC NK2004.3.F365 A4 2020 | DDC 747.092--dc23
LC record available at https://lccn.loc.gov/2020021850

Printed and bound in China by 1010 Printing International Limited

SECOND PRINTING